These Heavy
Black Bones

Rebecca Achieng Ajulu-Bushell

These Heavy
Black Bones

CANONGATE

First published in Great Britain in 2024
by Canongate Books Ltd, 14 High Street, Edinburgh EH1 1TE

canongate.co.uk

1

British Library Cataloguing-in-Publication Data
A catalogue record for this book is available on
request from the British Library

ISBN 978 1 80530 044 1

Typeset in Garamond by Palimpsest Book Production Ltd,
Falkirk, Stirlingshire

Printed and bound by CPI Group (UK) Ltd, Croydon CRO 4YY

MIX
Paper | Supporting
responsible forestry
FSC
www.fsc.org
FSC® C171272

For the little brown girl with the focused eyes, float easy, I've got you.

CONTENTS

Author's note   ix

Prologue   1

PART I: SWELL

Prepare

I   11

II   19

Develop

III   27

IV   36

V   44

VI   55

VII   64

VIII   73

Intensify

IX   82

X   91

XI   99

XII   109

PART 2: SUBSIDE

Taper

XIII   123

XIV   132

XV   141

XVI   150

Race

XVII   159

XVIII   170

XIX   177

XX   187

XXI   197

Recover

XXII   205

XXIII   215

XXIV   224

Epilogue   235

Acknowledgements   245

Author's Note

Swimming was one of the greatest loves of my young life. And like all love, I suffered for it. The act of remembering (suffering) is complex and the truth is slippery. Contained in this book is my story and I wrote it not to unearth anyone else's, but so I no longer bear the responsibility of remembering it alone, now I share that with you.

All the names in this book are pseudonyms and some of the characters have been adapted for narrative purposes.

Prologue

'I am no prophet – and here's no great matter;
I have seen the moment of my greatness flicker,
And I have seen the eternal Footman hold my coat,
and snicker,
And in short, I was afraid.'

T.S. Eliot

I didn't know bitterness until I had to step into the shadow of my own achievements, then watch someone else achieve what I believed should have been mine. It had been almost a year since my final race and every day after I had woken up disbelieving; squeezing my eyes shut and willing myself back into the dream, only when you fall asleep again the dream isn't the same – you can't get back to the place you want to be. Now, here in my room, I felt as fragile as if that race was yesterday, a sickness and a rage that tasted like chlorinated betrayal. I felt like walking through my house and systematically smashing everything. Instead, I sat. My cream-coloured bedsheets beneath me, slightly yellower than the cream-coloured carpet on the floor that blended seamlessly into the walls, the TV throwing static down the stairs. I opened the window to hear it better. Shrill and circus-like, the commentator was giving background on the event as one by one they walked out, and I could imagine the camera panning round to rest for a moment behind the starting blocks of each lane. Their race was about to start. I wanted to close the window to stop the sound of cheers erupting into my room after the announcement of each competitor's name and country; it was like looking directly at the sun. But I couldn't. I didn't want to watch but I couldn't miss it either. Listening felt like a bearable compromise; I knew exactly what it looked like: after all, I was supposed to be there.

The perfect race will haunt you forever. I didn't know that – there are so many things they don't tell you. For example: that when it's over for you it's over, immediately. Just like that. Worse still is that it doesn't stop: the next season rolls on without you like you never existed; the next competition happens like they had never announced your name at any competition before and you're left alone to drag yourself away from the wreckage. That you'll shred your cartilage into nothing after so many years of repetition and wake up in the night years later dripping in sweat with your shins on fire, phantom pains shooting through your hips. That you'll lose your mind, and you won't realise until it's truly gone – you've forgotten what your comfort zone ever felt like and all your memories are a disorganised chaos. But the perfect race is eternal, like an embarrassment so acute you see it every time you close your eyes and feel it every time your mind wanders too far. I could replay it over and over, flawlessly, my moment of ecstasy. I held it close, like an addict, and relived it whenever I could bear to, careful not to use it up. But sometimes it came to me in a flash, a feeling, triggered by a sound or the smell of chlorine in a garden centre. I never resisted because secretly I feared that the feeling was gone forever, and that a lifetime, *my* lifetime, might pass me by without my ever getting to feel it again.

*

Two sharp, clipped trills. I step forward, tension coursing through the arms as I think about lacing my fingers around the front of the board, waiting for the second whistle. I was perfect and I knew exactly when it would come. One long whistle followed. Exhale. I step up, slamming my right foot into the adjustable wedge at the back; slowly I transfer my weight forward, lowering my head, using its weight to bring everything I am into the ball of my left foot. Poised. Every muscle in my body tightens. I always close my eyes now, my Black genes twitching as I imagine the line marshal: he's lifting his hand in slow motion, he holds his arm out gesturing sideways to the starter, we are under his control. The start marshal lifts the microphone to his mouth, I'm playing out every move, his left thumb comes down slowly, I think I can hear the button click. Silence. Inhale. 'Take your marks,' he bellows, with long, drawn-out vowels. I empty all the thoughts from my mind, the ones I know and all the ones I don't, every training session, every instruction, every practice, every length, gone gone down down. I empty my whole mind to forget. My body doesn't need my brain for this, so I let go, until I am only a body and nothing more, sinew, muscle, rippling brown skin taut and stretched over my small, too-short-to-be-a-sprint-swimmer-body. I forget my family, my friends, my coach, my name: I forget everything that makes me worry, forget everything that makes you human. The buzzer sounds, I spring. They are still on the blocks.

The silence at the start of the race is almost religious. The stadium is church-like, its congregation hangs from the stands. And everyone, every person, is looking at you, in the very middle, furthest away from the wake that slows you down as it hits the edge of the pool: lane four. If you haven't already psyched yourself out in the call room, or in warm-up, or with a shaky heat swim in the morning, or a rip in your racing costume, this moment will finish you off. It's a silence so pure and pregnant most can't prepare through it, because in that silence you can hear your heartbeat thumping in your ears, it threatens to sever the connection between your brain and your limbs. But that's how you win: you beat the silence, because after it, there's only noise. My body arches faultlessly and for a moment I am completely still in the air, feeling the hyperextension of my shoulders as they hold my head in place, drawing a line to the tips of my fingernails. Just as my body starts to fall, I flick a wave of motion from my hips, my chin drops a couple of centimetres and my straight body, which I have just flung headlong off the blocks, aiming for the flags, tilts forward. My fingers hit the water. A small porthole, no bigger than the circumference of my swimming hat, ripples out from this contact, and through it I disappear below the surface.

Counting happens without effort, streamlined under the

4

water. I wait. Allowing the nothing to envelop me. One. Two. Pull. It's the moment just before the moment I start to feel myself slowing down. An instinct to keep moving forward, something in a prehistoric part of my brain concerned only with inertia. As my arms pull downward, travelling in deliberate lines to my side, grazing my chest, I sense their perfect communion with the water, my wrists twisting imperceptibly, even to me, as my hands create and escape the resistance of this liquid world. This part is like the dream within a dream, I know I'm coming up soon, but I can't rush, nor stay here any longer than I should. There is a lot of discipline needed to leave this place, so quiet and so smooth. The muscles that frame the top of my pelvis are straining. I kick from the bottom of my stomach to my ankles, like a shiver, and my soft feet move in response. Soft feet, soft hands, tight body, hard mind. My knees are yearning to part, and I hold on to the very last millisecond. I'm only 5 centimetres below the surface now and I start to let my lungs guide me up. The first breaststroke kick. Snap heels back, push hips down, flex feet, pull elbows in. Drive: legs backward, arms forward. I'm reaching with my body, reaching up to the shallows. I'm here. I can already hear it. I break the surface and fill my lungs with electricity, oxygenating my blood with the sound of a thousand people cheering.

The stroke count is right. Fifty metres pass me by like a landscape past a train window. I know I'm ahead, but I only have this thought when I'm replaying it, in the moment all my training stops me from entertaining this distraction. I reject the comfort of the wall; my hands retract immediately as I hit the touchpad with all my power. My body contracts. Knees towards forehead, feet towards the unmovable object in front of me. Keeping my body small, I twist from my waist and my intercostal muscles turn all my mass on an axis. With every moment I spend here I lose energy to the wall, all the speed I've gained down this first length of the pool is being sucked away from me into the concrete and tiles. I move quickly now to keep some of this energy within me so I can force it in the opposite direction. Drive. Back to my underwater world and back up again. The air is hotter in my mouth as I suck it down into my chest, my lungs getting smaller and smaller with each breath. I make it a further 25 metres before parts of my conscious brain start to come back to me, the fear reawakens my mind and I can't believe I've made it this far without it. Don't seize up, don't seize up. There's no one around me and I'm not slowing down. How am I not slowing down? 'Shut up,' I tell myself. It arrives.

Lactic acid floods my veins, rushing from my thighs up towards my shoulders, consuming every muscle in its path. Pain unimaginable: ribbons and rivers of white fury devouring every drop of oxygen in my bloodstream. But with it something else too. Slowly, everything begins to melt into the background, becoming the bits of a painting that are too far away to have any details, soft, fuzzy trees on a hilltop far away. Everything is fuzzy and far away, everything except this new warmth. It's spreading from my sternum, coating my body in joy, I'm lifted. I think I'm smiling now. Gliding and floating, and this time my body leaves me instead, wrapped in euphoria, my favourite music and my mother's voice. I can just about hear the dull, faraway sound of cheers. I feel no pain. And the water isn't wet because my body is not here. I'm smiling still. I look for the wall, it's so close. Everything is perfect and nothing hurts. The motion I know better than any other is carrying me under the 5-metre flags. I squeeze my forearms together, and one last breaststroke kick pulls my hips up and forward. Hyperextended from my shoulder blades to my knuckles, the tiny arena on the very end of my middle fingers meets the wall and I know the clock has stopped. Slowly my broad brown hands come into my view and I'm still moving forward but it's over. In a split second all my world comes back to me, my body comes back to myself, and everything goes black. I lift my head out of the water and look upward at the scoreboard, at the very same moment the background leaps forward, the wetness of the water, the noise, the colours, the pain, everything bursts into technicolour.

PART I

Swell

Prepare

I

'I – have always carried deep
these islands,
this piece of Atlantic coastland
inside me.'

Grace Nichols

I'm underwater with my eyes open, pensive and still. I've always had the feeling of being underwater; it's where most of my childhood happened. Pensive and waiting for my life to begin: for the bubbles to show me a route to the surface, or for the air in my lungs to run out. But there was a time before I knew the exquisite pain of taking a hit of water straight to the brain, the oxygen in my sinuses beckoning it after I dive in as the pressure difference pushes it up and through my nose. Before I knew the water as my home, I knew the uncertainty of a childhood spent moving constantly, coupled with the certainty of my mother's love; and disappointment was a distant promise that I couldn't yet pronounce. We moved all the time and so did I, my body dancing through the days. They went by so quickly in my childhood, fast because they were so rich; not like the modern classics about coming of age in a nowhere place where nothing happens. Everything happened in my childhood. Before anything else, before I was even born, the first thing to happen was my father leaving. In a quiet pain I didn't understand or explore until much later, I grew up with my mother, and later my stepfather; and all the other people who had been brought into our orbit by a twenty-something white single mum in the early '90s with a mixed-race baby and student loans. She grew up poor on a council estate in Runcorn, a sprawling hell of concrete between Liverpool and Manchester, with a father who I never met; she wouldn't let him near any of us, my younger sisters and me. I was distanced too by my father's new marriage, my birth too close and my face too much like my father's for anyone to be confused about what had happened.

My mother had me young; she met my father when they were both teaching at a university. He was a professor of politics, very Black, very smart, very indulgent. His greatest indulgence was helping people he didn't know. By the time I was born my father had been in and out of prison multiple times, politically exiled from his homeland, Kenya, and led student resistance movements all across Africa. It was almost 1994, and in South Africa, where my father had studied, the African National Congress (ANC) – Nelson Mandela's newly reformed political party – was about to take power. My birth coincided with the fall of the apartheid regime and my father leaving for this new South Africa, for the liberation of his people, and because, I've since learned, my mother told him that if it felt like a choice he shouldn't stay. A freedom baby: I've heard people say that about me. I used to think it was because of when I was born but realised later it was also *what* I was born. A breathing blend of my parents' skin, a squishy emblem of progress. Brown and in-between. Hair in-between, not big and beautiful like the hair belonging to the girls with deep blue hues in their high cheekbones, nor flicky and light and pullable, cascading down my back. Just in-between. Body also in-between. I was a strong, thin child, not short, not tall, naturally athletic from my first moments, African muscles but no African curves. My reactions were fast and clear in the way they communicated my wants and needs to my arms and legs; anything I tried, my body moved how I told it to.

In Reading, where my mother and I lived when I was three years old after returning from a small village in Malawi near the border of Mozambique, I used to ride a small yellow and red scooter to my nursery school a couple of roads away. We went to live in that small village in East Africa so my mother could do her PhD research. We came back because she couldn't really afford to do a PhD, and rented a small, terraced house from a man who would later become my stepfather. In the house there were pictures of me back in Malawi washing my small naked body in a shallow plastic bucket in the backyard. The earth is red, and the bucket is red, and I am smiling. I had no sense of struggle, or the debt my mother was in; I only knew her love and her hands, reaching down to lift me into her bed at one in the morning when I would reach up to her with chubby fingers, finished playing with my multi-coloured wooden blocks because sleep had finally found me. On the back of the bathroom door, she had Blu-Tacked a poster of the flags of the world; everything was for learning. That's how it started. My mother, who grew up with so little love around her, wanted to bathe me in it; she washed me in it every day, she read it to me every night, she loved me so hard it hurt.

Competitiveness, like all things, is a practice. But I was born with it baked in, a head start, a small beast locked in a too-small cage, snarling at the bars whenever there was a task at hand. My mother started feeding it young. Maybe she recognised I was easy to motivate that way, or she wanted the little beast to break free and help me grow big and strong. Maybe, in birthing me she'd learned what my father had always known: that I might have to work twice as hard to have half as much. I walked early, I talked early, I read early. My mother read *A Midsummer Night's Dream* to me and she would help me memorise verses; we played 'name the flags of the world' on the toilet. Knowledge was just a challenge, a game to be won. My early years were flash cards and breastmilk; I gorged on my mother's love; it never ran out. As she poured it into me, we grew up and together. I was a piece of her rib; she was my left arm. She made me strong, loved, smart, entitled, a winner.

Soon we would move to Kenya for good, but for a short

time before that my mother and I travelled around Uganda. She was doing research while a junior lecturer at a university back in the UK. We would always fly through South Africa first and she would take me to see my father. His house smelled of another woman's perfume, and my older brother, his first-born son, was there. He got upset when our father took phone calls, I didn't understand why until later. My father had traded revolution for revelry. Marrying into a political dynasty in South Africa, his new life in Pretoria was shrouded by jacaranda trees and mining money. My mother's devotion to me – that I should know him – kept us all connected as he receded into this inaccessible world.

'Where did you get that baby?' People would ask my mum in the back of matatus back in Uganda. There were chickens strapped to the roof, a private shared taxi you paid a couple of shillings for, and they stopped whenever needed, spray-painted with Liverpool football club's anthem 'You'll Never Walk Alone'. People hung out the side and carried small animals on their heads but none of this was out of place; nothing was as strange as the beautiful, tall, tanned white woman in the back with a brown baby on her breast. I had my third birthday in Uganda and that weekend we went down to Lake Victoria. With armbands, a floaty vest and a rubber ring on I would get in so long as my mother never let me go. My ancestors learned to be in communion with the water here, on the shores of Lake Victoria, and so would I. My father was Luo, a tribe of East African fishermen, proud and political – Obama's father was Luo too. Eventually it was time and I floated; the inflated plastic swaddling me had kept only my fears at the surface. My mother took away her hands and the water became my home.

After we moved to Nairobi to be with my stepfather, he said I could keep one of the new puppies from the litter his dog had just birthed. He told me I could name them all too. My dad, as I called him, and as he became, wanted my mother so much that he also wanted me. I named all the puppies after herbs except mine, which I called Pip. His house was a beautiful sprawl, all on one floor, white and terracotta up a long driveway and a lawn that sloped down towards the hedge through which our dogs dragged the neighbours' dog one night and killed it. The neighbours were three Kenyan nuns; we gave them one of our dogs, Basil, in recompense.

My stepfather went to university at seventeen, he knew everything, and still does, and then he lived in Nepal before buying some land in the Kenyan highlands and settling into the humanitarian world. He planned for drought and disaster, how to get rice to remote places in the middle of a war. The first four years of my life it was just adults, and I still had another three to go before my first sister was born, but now I had the outside, the sunshine, and I knew what passionfruit flowers looked like. My toes were stubbed and bloody for most of these years and the landscape of scars on my shins that got worse in the gym years later was first marked in this garden climbing trees and walking barefoot, falling over hot stones and acacia thorns. My stepfather gave me an art room and filled it with patience, and in that time, he also became my parent. A small light-filled atrium at the back of the house with tall glass letterbox windows. Among the boxes of coloured paper and glitter glue was glass paint. I squatted by the lowest row of the windowpanes, selected a square and painted small blue dolphins on the glass with him. My tails were puffy and misshapen, his were angular and fish-like. We would stay like this together for hours, painting other things that swam, building dams and throwing balls.

Over long weekends we took the one-hour flight from Nairobi to Mombasa. At the coast, I would spend almost eight hours a day between the pool and the Indian Ocean; my cornrows grew fuzzy after only a couple of days and my skin was dark sepia against my bright pink rash vest. Weekends were spent like this, making mermaids out of white sand on the long beaches and finding kelp for their hair and two fish eggs for eyes. Or we would pack into my stepfather's second-hand 4x4 and drive up-country to Naivasha, camping with my parents' friends and their children. Zebras became commonplace on these drives, giraffes too; years later, when I moved back to England, I found hedgehogs and badgers exotic, strange and rare by comparison. When I started kindergarten in Nairobi, I was moved up a year. I was four years old, and I started doing 25-metre swimming races at school galas. 'I predict she'll be a swimming star of the future', the head of the sports department wrote in my report at the end of that first term. Subconsciously, I was getting ready. The bus to school was an hour each way each day. I mostly stayed in my thoughts apart from one morning when I saw a man who had been on a bicycle hit by a car in the road. The handlebar went through his stomach. I was scared of my imagination; it felt endless, like the deepest bath, and when I cried – which was seldom – my tears wouldn't stop coming, it was like I was leaking. A sadness I held inside me fell from my lids, and like Alice in Wonderland I thought I would drown myself in salty tears, a pool of fear. I never remembered what I was crying about when it was over, only that I couldn't stop; and sometimes I would cry myself to sleep, at the hairdressers' getting too-tight-braids, three aunties pulling at my little pale scalp.

II

Until I turned six, I had celebrated every birthday in a different country. I envied the kids whose lives were static, but after a couple of years in Kenya, life had started to settle for me too. I had a best friend who lived next door and went to the same school as me. It was a serious place; my classmates were clever, and although my reading age was still advanced, after a childhood of being applauded for my intelligence, academically I could feel myself becoming ordinary. In response, I turned to sport; I moved every day, tennis, rounders, athletics, hockey and swimming. There was an upstairs to our new house and my room had a tiny inside window that looked onto the stairwell. My mother always knew when I was reading late. I still slept very little, just the same as when I was a baby, and read endlessly; by torch light, under the covers, with my lamp on and heart pounding, turning it off as soon as I heard a creak somewhere else in the house. Sometimes I read too late even for me, and the fear would creep through the window and wrap itself around my bedposts. I would stand outside my parents' room in the early hours of the morning. Too scared to go in, because I couldn't put words to my fear, or why I was standing there, too scared to go back to sleep, scared of what I would find in my dreams and behind my eyelids.

My mother and stepfather got married in Tanzania just after my sixth birthday. Gold and cream flowers embroidered on an ivory raw silk bodice with a wide gold sash and matching shoes from Accessorize or Monsoon. My hair was puffy. I was so upset by it the morning of the ceremony that my mother's best friend washed it out for me again in the bath and blow-dried it straight. It was puffy still, but I read my poem and only faltered once, surrounded by 10,000 white roses. Then, my sister was born. And I understood that although it would be impossible to stop my mother and me from being two parts of one body, my relationship with this family was forever changed. They were a family, and I was me. I was untethered – no longer the sole child that made my parents a family – and finally having to face that, in some way, that had always been a fallacy.

My sister's birth led me back to an early childhood relation-ship. I turned to my first carer, eager to push against his world and prove that I really was on the outside. My mother had left home at seventeen; education was her way out. She needed to finish school and to do that she needed get as far away from her abusive father as possible. A little later, after her final exams, she moved in with her then boyfriend, Paul; he was charismatic, gruff, Northern, cynical education hadn't been his way. He had a silver tooth at the front of his mouth with a smiley face on it and strange, anarchic stick-and-poke tattoos on his calves. He was a cameraman, at first filming extreme sports. Strapped into the front of a kayak he'd be ploughing through white water or set up on the Isle of Man at the side of a racetrack as bikes passed by a fingernail away, and later music, live tours, all the people you've heard of. By the time I was born they hadn't been a couple for a long while, but when my mother had to go back to work, they had looked after me together. He was my first dad, a love of my young life. I think they tried to be a family, but they were already going to different places. He would come and visit us when we moved out to Kenya. Taking me away from him broke everyone's heart a little, my mother's most of all. By the time I was six or seven I would fly back to the UK by myself to see him, wearing brushed-cotton teddy-bear pyjamas in dark blue, an unaccompanied minor on a British Airways overnight to Heathrow. He had a new partner, and I knew they would get married soon and have their own children, but we walked on pebbled beaches together, just me and him, in Brighton. Sometimes he took me to Disneyland Paris even though I don't know if he could afford to, and I wore a purple Esmeralda dress, the only brown princess.

I found some part of my identity through this newfound singularity. I was interested in the idea that I was somehow alone. As I grew into the personality this offered up to me, I found myself performing a confidence I didn't really have. I was never a classic introvert; I was just very intense, and because of this, I didn't do very well at talking to children when I was much younger. I was intense about everything, and I only felt at ease with people I could be intense with. This was often mistaken for arrogance, so much so that it started to become that; I was a leader, sometimes a bully, captain of the hockey, rounders, athletics and netball teams, school plays, school councils. I realised success made people like you more, or at least respond to you differently; in the classroom, on the pitch, in the pool. By now I was also competing every weekend. Our first competition, we knew nothing: not when to line up for the race, or how many whistles there were at the start. I couldn't dive, I didn't know that I had to touch the wall with two hands for butterfly or breaststroke, but my mum wrote down everything. Every instruction, every heat, the fastest times, who was swimming them. She would swim with me, sitting in the hot concrete stands rocking and pushing herself forward from the hips every time my head broke the surface. 'Swim, Achi swim, swim, Achi swim.' That was the sound of my childhood.

I hadn't yet read Toni Morrison but when my second sister was born, I became obsessed with blue eyes. I wanted to peel off my skin, a cage my two sisters kept me in; I would be so much better at being white than they were. And I would step out of this brown disguise with long dark hair and light eyes and lighter skin, and I would be desirable in the way that my mother was, in the way I understood beauty. It wasn't about belonging – to my white family, or to the universality of whiteness around me – it was just a reflection of how I saw the world reflected at me, and how I wanted to be in it. Our move to South Africa made this desire stronger: I liked my hair wet because it was straighter that way; I liked my skin less tanned because it was lighter like that.

There was a very white international school close to where we lived. When we went to visit, the headmistress told us she just had a burning desire to do something about the lack of diversity. I would have been the only student of colour. I was ten and though I hadn't heard anything racialised like that before, I understood what she was saying, and I thought it was bullshit. My mum wouldn't send me there, so instead I went to a very mixed but very colonial government school where we wore regulation underwear, knee-high socks and straw hats. I wasn't allowed to have my hair braided, but there were other brown faces in my class. The other swimmers became my community. Training was a very different place from my hours spent in school. Most of the swimmers were brown, Black, Cape Coloured; they went to all different schools and had all different backgrounds, but we came together in the water. I had outgrown the swimming world of Nairobi but when I moved to Cape Town, I had to wear flippers all session for the first couple of months just to keep up. We trained in a 50-metre pool that had an inflatable dome over it to keep it warm through the cooler winter months. There had only been one 50-metre pool in Nairobi, and it was always green.

My mother eventually caved, worn down both by my complaining that I wasn't learning anything except for how to write in cursive and all the driving around: the hour back and forth across the mountain to school each morning after an hour back and forth to training before that followed by another hour back and forth to training in the evening, and then the pick-ups. I moved to the white international school and a boy kicked me in the stomach; I still have a faint scar down the soft part of my tummy under my ribs. Teachers asked me if I was adopted, parents accused me of being in the year above, a cheat, because I was too good at hockey to only be twelve, and I got my first and last detention for correcting my teacher. 'Orangutan doesn't have a g at the end,' I'd told her. – 'Not so clever now, are you?' she said as I ran from the classroom crying.

As we were both in South Africa, I thought I would see my father more, but I remember I just spent a lot of time waiting for him. When he did come, he brought my younger brother in a blacked-out government car with flags on the front of it and a phone in the armrest of the back seat. I was competing in Joburg once and we went out for dinner with his wife's children, his new son and my older brother. This was a family. My mother was with me, and I could feel the hot tears collecting in the corners of my eyes as I watched them sit easily in their shared upbringing. I ran to the toilet and by the time she found me next to the hand dryer they were falling down my cheeks. Years later I found out that we all went to that same school in Cape Town for a while.

When my sister was nearly three, she almost drowned. I found her slightly submerged under the water in the pool in our garden, floating on her back, her face a pale blue, a little grey, like cheap-looking fish, and her eyes were rolled back into her head. I shouted, to make real the unreality of that moment, and jumped into the water. I pulled her out to the side as my mother and grandmother came running, then lay on my back next to her on the grass while my grandmother did CPR and we waited for her to breathe. My mother was screaming. After an eternity of seconds my sister started coughing and we went to the hospital; my parents told me I couldn't let her fall asleep and so I told her long and never-ending stories as I let my mind float away from her and the incident to settle instead on the water. The Atlantic Ocean on our doorstep had taught me that my liquid home had no intention of being careful with me. My fear of the water was so rational that it wasn't even a fear at all, it was humility, so much so that I was quietly unsurprised that my sister had almost lost her life in this smaller body of water in our back garden. Out beyond the waves, swaying on my surfboard, I had felt how easily that battle could be lost, so easily that the water wouldn't even feel you fight. The open ocean is the most demanding, but all water demands things from you: it demands communion and reverence, but mostly it demands knowledge.

My mum wasn't working the three years we lived in Cape Town, which made her restless, and more able to feel scared about raising three girls in a place that felt, at times, very dangerous. And slowly I started to feel her worries too. I didn't know how to be in a place that felt so hard and angry as this. Who was I? Strange European features on a caramel-coloured face, and a stranger transatlantic twang to my international school accent, peppered with Afrikaans slang. I tried, but I didn't fit. Then, just before I turned thirteen, my mother got offered a big job back in Kenya and I came back from the South African age-group Nationals with a heavy bunch of medals.

Moving back to Kenya meant the end of progress for my training, it meant no more indoor pools and no more Eastern-Bloc coach and no more exposure to swimmers better than me. Earlier in the year Mum had taken me to try out at swimming schools in England, all boarding, all in the south-west. At the first school the coach offered me a scholarship after three strokes. Then we went to see the fancy school that everyone knew. The other swimmers watched my trial session from the balcony almost jeering. I had never seen anything like it; there was a helicopter pad and under the stench of chlorine was the stronger smell of new middle-class wealth. Their pool was amazing, sparkling; some mornings before training in South Africa, we had to shoo the ducks off before we got in. At the last school I met Roan, the towering coach of an up-and-coming club that had just paired with a sports school. He took me and my mum to Costa and sat in a plastic leather armchair across from me. 'Why should I come here?' I asked him. 'Because I'll make you the best,' he replied simply. Roan didn't need to say much. His whole being exuded confidence. By the end of that summer, it had been decided. My dad got on a plane and took my sisters back to Kenya; my mum and I got on a plane and flew to the UK.

Develop

III

*'If you see me lost in neglected
woods, I'm no thief eyeing trees
to plunder their stability
or a moaner shouting at air'*

James Berry

The swimmers' boarding house was on the same site as the primary school and also an old prison. There were small residential homes within the private complex which stood inside a very tall, thick stone wall, an old naval base, rebuilt after the war. The boarding house itself was exactly like this too, an old stone building with worn pillars either side of the double doorway at the front. The girls were on the top floor and the boys on the bottom. Each floor had its own little common room, a kitchen, a couple of sets of bathrooms, some with showers, some with toilets, some with both, the matron's room, and double and single rooms, all with single beds. There were a handful of assistant coaches in their mid-twenties who lived in the boarding house too; one was our house mistress, who used sarcasm to cover up her own insecurities. She always wore three-quarter-length leggings and a fitted gym polo, sometimes with a hoodie, and her hair pulled back in a tight, short pony-tail with a deep parting. It was a very English place, with thin, worn carpets and sofas salvaged from British Heart Foundation, straight out of a '70s living room.

If you were in the first session on a Saturday morning – up before 6 a.m., a lie-in compared to the weekday sessions, which started just after 5 a.m. – you could come back to the boarding house and watch TV in the main common room. The boys came up the back stairwell, a metal fire escape on the outside of the building that connected the ground floor to the edge of the first. The heavy fire door opened into a small corridor with boys' toilets on the left before spilling into a larger area, the main corridor, that led to the shared common room. There were lots of doors, the kind that swing back and forth inde-pendently, and the whole building felt like an old children's hospital, clinical and stark. To get from the boarding house to school and also to training, there was a white minibus with staggered seating and seatbelts rising from the grey felt roof. The drive out of the Millfields, as it was called, took you through the whole base, around the churchyard and through perfectly manicured green glades that sloped down towards the road banked with oak trees. There was a small security office at the main gate surrounded by matt green awning and hanging baskets with sad wildflowers wilting over their edges. Everything was alien to me. A white-haired man with a thick Plymothian accent manned the boom gate and Graige Drive opened immediately onto a council estate called Clarence Court; we turned left here. Beyond that was a Lidl and beyond that a bus that took you into town.

The school was about a fifteen-minute drive away, on the other side of the city. The rain was extreme: it came down sideways from the moors and as it rushed towards the sea to be once again connected with its end, it coated the city in sheets of water. Rihanna's 'Umbrella' played constantly on Heart FM and Radio 1Xtra, and the minibus often parked at the front of the school outside the reception, an ugly cream building with white window-frames. The school was made up of lots of disparate parts that had all been tacked on at different periods over the last couple of hundred years. There was the old school building, a once beautiful but now depressing grey Tudor castle whose floors were dark and more polish than wood, with wide staircases that ran up both sides of the building to the language department. The dining hall sat in the heart of the grounds with a covered courtyard leading up three steps to multiple entranceways where different year groups would line up ahead of lunch. The courtyard was flagstoned and tables were scattered near the back where people sat for first break. It was surrounded by other subject buildings, the Classics and Latin block, science labs and a corridor of English classrooms. A relatively underwhelming 25-metre pool sat in an old sports centre. Underwhelming, I observed, considering that in this country there seemed to be a heated 25-metre indoor pool everywhere. It wasn't a school where you called teachers sir, but even the Head of Sports was addressed in full. The girls' changing rooms at the sports centre felt like a crypt: a cold, damp, windowless space, the site of a thousand tears and mean-girl triumphs. It had a permanent uncleanliness to it, not that it wasn't cleaned, just that it could never be clean. Either you walked barefoot through the showers onto poolside, and it was disgusting, or you wore a slider and you were considered a freak: only international students wore slip-ons in the changing room – outsiders, as I would come to know them.

All the girls had long hair, which they wore very straight and smelled a little bit of burning. If it wasn't a very pale straw-blonde, it was a dark plum colour: not rich, just black with a purple hue, sometimes a blue-black, even. Make-up was liberally applied everywhere above the jawline. A moussey, cakey, dessert-like foundation blended into the hairline with shadows of burnt-orange bronzing powder forehead, cheek and nose. Eyeliner blended with a mascara that never came off, in a dark hyper-contrasted line around the outer two-thirds of the bottom and top eyelids. The look came together with a washed-out lip, the foundation was buffed into the cupid's bow and down on to the rosebud of the mouth and then coated with lip balm, usually not gloss. 'You're pretty,' a girl with very blonde hair and very dark eye make-up announced. 'I'm going to call you Pretty from now on.' I smiled very small and said thank you in a surprisingly tiny voice that echoed how I felt about being the new girl but more about being called pretty, which I didn't believe I could be, despite knowing that I was. We were standing in the courtyard and the bell had just rung for first break; it was my first day and Nicole's words buoyed me.

I had arrived in Plymouth in late August in a dark grey Superdry T-shirt with a crimson motif of the number 52 on the back. My mum took photos of me in front of the boarding house after we unpacked the car. There was another new girl in my year, Amelia, and we were to share a room at the front of the house, on the side nearest the shared common room. I liked her as soon as we met. My bed was tucked into the corner and the walls were periwinkle with corkboards that had horrible silver rims hung above the beds for pictures and posters.

That first day of school I had morning training – up at 4.45 a.m. and onto the bus, then into the pool for 5.30 for a two-hour session. Amelia and I ate breakfast in five minutes so we could get ready properly in the non-swimming boarding house. I did a green eyeshadow with a bit of glitter to match our green, red, and black tartan skirts and black blazer with green twirled trim. Taking care to make it as unbulky as possible, I rolled my skirt up at the waistband; that's universal. 'It doesn't matter if you're a bit late for your form tutor,' one of the older girls told us. 'You just tell them you're a swimmer and they won't even mark you up.' Amelia and I were in the same tutor group. As well as being roommates, we were the same age, which meant we would live together, eat together, train together, learn together and race together. Against each other.

It was a long day of trying not to draw the wrong kind of attention to myself. The blonde girl who had called me pretty, Nicole, was in my form as well and when we went back to our tutor group after lunch, she sat next to me as our tutor handed out our lesson schedules as well as our set assignments. I was in second set for Maths and Science but first for English; I didn't understand why but assumed I would find out.

'So what school were you at before this?' She turned her peroxide head towards me as she asked. After I explained that my family lived in Kenya, but I'd just moved from Cape Town, she just screwed up her face a little and her small nose wrinkled at the bridge and then she didn't ask me any more questions. I looked over to Amelia and saw that she was talking to a boy, holding her hair all to one side of her head and running both hands down its length. She was talking to the boy in the same way the blonde girls back in Cape Town had, in a way I didn't seem to be able to. My accent sounded increasingly foreign as I watched them, and every time I thought about speaking, I was scared I would say something strange. 'It's true,' Amelia was saying, 'no, it really is true . . .' She was laughing, more like a giggle, and the boy said something back to her but he had his back to me so I couldn't make it out. The bell rang and I felt very glad as I put my lesson plan into my diary and put it into my canvas tote bag. My feet were a little wet, maybe because I wore flat pumps and they were never really dry, but also because of the near-constant rain. It collected in deceptively deep puddles around the steps at the bottom of the sports centre.

It was 3.37 p.m. and I was early. I sat down on the thin wooden-slatted bench that ran the circumference of the changing rooms next to my swimming bag and let the pebble-dash walls and strip lighting keep me company. My costume still wasn't dry after morning training and I thought about my permanently wet feet, the fact that I'd already been up almost twelve hours, and the two-hour threshold set ahead of me. 'This set is gonna be so rough.' It was the older girl from that morning, and she was speaking to another new girl; Kayli came through the door just after her. 'I'm so fucking unfit, honestly I feel like I'm just gonna sink immediately,' she said. Kayli was beautiful – tall, tanned, soft brown hair framing soft brown eyes and pared-back make-up. She was already in sixth form. I turned in the corner where I was sitting, and with my back to both of them, I started to unbutton my school shirt. I kept it over my shoulders as I pulled my tights down under my skirt and then slipped my underwear off to follow, standing my bare feet on my slightly damp pumps. I pulled my costume off my bag – in the morning I had seen the other girls looping their costumes through the strap at the top of their bags and then pulling the suit through the gusset to secure it and let it dry, and I'd copied. Quickly, I stepped into my costume and in a single motion I pulled it up under my skirt, dropped one of my arms from my shirt sleeve and slipped the strap of my costume onto my right shoulder and then, as my shirt fell, my left. I went from uniform to swimming costume in less than thirty seconds and without exposing myself at all. I had been getting changed on poolside having full conversations with male coaches for years.

The boys were loud, as if they had all already made friends even though some of them were as new as I was. We could hear them in their changing room as we walked past the showers and out onto poolside. Our kit bags were all at the far end so you had to come out of the changing rooms and turn right, walk all the way to the end of the pool, find your bag, make sure all your kit was in your bag, and then carry your bag the length of the pool back up to the top, where there was a huge whiteboard and diving blocks put in behind each lane. I had no boobs, no hips, no bum, lots of muscle, my shoulders were getting broad, and I felt incredibly self-conscious as the light spilled through the floor-to-ceiling windows onto my thirteen-year-old body, casting shadows on my thighs as I walked down the far side of the pool. 'Jenkins, Jenkins!' Dan was shouting at one of the boys in his deep Northern accent as he walked out of the changing rooms. Dan was the kind of boy who could make anyone do anything: his face was perfectly symmetrical, and his mod-style short back and sides haircut meant he looked like he'd stepped straight out of a Stone Island ad. His left ear was pierced and the soft, downy hair on the bottom half of his abs turned blond to brown as it disappeared into his trunks. Kayli was one of the last to come onto poolside, at the very same time that Roan, the head coach, pushed open the door from the sports centre at the topmost turn of the pool. Everyone turned to look at him and he watched Kayli walk the far length of the pool with her kit bag, her hips swinging slowly from side to side; his tongue came slowly out of the right-hand corner of his mouth, darting and wet as he moistened his lips to speak,

'Costumes don't shrink, you know!' he bellowed at her.

IV

When I started swimming a lot, around the age of nine, I cut my impossible-to-control hair short, a cropped bob that sat 8 centimetres below my ears. Already chlorine-damaged and kinky, I tied it up always, and instead of getting it braided or spending any real time caring for it, I convinced my mum – after years of screaming and hiding matted clumps in the weeks leading up to my hair appointments – to let me get it relaxed. Chemically straightened. Ammonium thioglycolate: a strong alkali that breaks the bonds in your African hair and eradicates the natural curl pattern. The process releases formaldehyde, the chemical used to preserve dead bodies. And when complete, the hair hangs straight and limp, sometimes a little spongy but with no real elasticity, relaxed.

Even though it was broken, it still had a volume that wouldn't cooperate. It never looked light and fluffy and pullable, it always looked heavy, oily, manipulated. Except for when it was wet. When my hair was wet it clung to my scalp – the wiry, chemically damaged strands weighed down by the water that gripped its lengths – just like the other girls, whose light, mousey hair looked dark brown after they'd taken off their swimming hats and slipped under the lane ropes, throwing their heads back so their hair sprayed, fan-like in the water as they pulled themselves out at the side of the pool. Water is the thing that Black hair needs more than anything else, the only true hydrator of its thirsty, dry coils. It is also the thing that returns it to its natural state, the state you spend your life avoiding. But not now: now, when it is wet, there is no difference; that's the best part about relaxed hair. The worst part about relaxed hair is regrowth. The first two weeks are perfect. I would treat my hair as white as I could: messy buns, take it down, put it up again, throw my head forward after training and flick my hair back then retie, undo, run my fingers through it. Until it dried and returned to its synthetic state. At three weeks I was less self-satisfied. It wouldn't sit quite as flat; imperceptibly – but not to me – half a centimetre of curl separated the wiry strands from my scalp now. By five weeks I would take the straighteners to the front of it, small sizzles hissed between the ceramic plates because it was still wet. Wet always. I fought it down and would sometimes put a thin ballet-pump-pink elastic headband on and push the front slick back. It would puff up after the band with a tiny duck's tail bun that sat in line with my ears at the back of my head, the ends sticking straight out and back.

I didn't yet know any Black people in Plymouth, not at

swimming nor in school. I didn't see them in town, or if I did, then they must have been invisible to me. There must've been Black people though, because in the big Boots near Drake Circus shopping centre they sold a couple of purple boxes of Dark & Lovely hair relaxer. In the corner of our room was a sink with a plyboard cupboard built around it and a cheap mirror on the wall and an old shaver light with a dirty pull-string. I tried to relax my hair in this privacy, over the sink, while my roommate was at late training; but the ventilation was so poor, and we weren't allowed to lock our doors. I felt exposed and anxious, as if one of the older girls were going to come in and ask me for a hairbrush or where Amelia was. Instead, I went to the big shower room at the far end of the floor near the matron's office, through the double doors, past the top of the staircase and through some double doors again.

It's almost impossible to relax your own hair without burning some part of your scalp. You only have twenty minutes to get all of the treatment onto your hair, equally, between small partings, smoothed in, and left to sit and then washed off again. You start from the coarsest, densest part, usually the crown or the nape of your neck where the curls are tight and constantly dry like a Brillo pad. Then you work to the fairest part of your hair, usually at the front or the edges that frame your face, where the hair that you like is soft and always moisturised and the curl pattern is looser. Four even sections of hair. Treatment only to the parts that haven't already received it. Just the regrowth, and not to your scalp either. In the days after the treatment, tiny pinprick scabs would form under my hair, pulling the skin on my head, already tight and itchy from being wet-dry-wet; I scratched, they flaked, but my hair was so straight that even though my scalp scared me I soon forgot. Eight weeks later I was ready to repeat the ritual, fingers fumbling in baggy plastic gloves with a metal-tailed comb touching the strong alkali chemical to my soft fleshy scalp as I applied it, blind, to the back of my hairline.

That first time, Amelia came into the shower room and started picking at her spots in the mirror. 'Oh my god,' she said immediately, 'Julia was *so* annoying this evening, you know when she like sings those songs and claps at you and puts her hands on your face.' She paused. 'It was only because I wasn't beating Lucy in the main set – and she calls me nicknames sometimes too. Anyway, are you almost done?'

'Yeah, almost,' I said. I was in one of the shower stalls and I couldn't see what I was doing but I didn't want her to see parts of the back of my hair half sticking up and my eyes streaming with salty tears. The relaxer had been on at least twenty-three minutes at the crown of my head now. I was quickly working my way through the front of my hair, smoothing my roots into my scalp with insistence. The insistence that they be straight, and this be over.

'Have you done your chemistry homework?' – 'Yeah, I did it in class today.' – 'Do you mind?' she said, mainly to herself in the mirror. 'No, it's fine, it's in my bag.' – 'Okay, I'll see you in a second,' Amelia sang out, and as I heard her pick up our bags I came out of the shower.

'Will you wait for me just two secs, I just need to wash this off?' I asked, almost desperately; doing anything alone, especially something like this, felt far too exposing.

'Yeah, but I really need to work, I'm gonna end up getting like one minute of sleep, and I have morning training and then chemistry first thing.'

Sara – the older girl from the changing rooms my first day – came in at that moment.

'Amelia, I was looking for you,' she started and looked my way for a second. '. . . You have an epilator, right?' she turned back to Amelia.

'Yep—'

'What the fuck is that smell?' Sara looked at me. 'It stinks of fish in here,' she spat and looked at both of us.

Amelia fiddled with the strap on her bag, and I turned and put the shower on. 'It's hair treatment,' I said and closed the shower door.

When I got back to our room Amelia was sitting at her desk; our desks were back-to-back and pushed together so we would face each other if we were working at the same time. She had my book open. She wasn't looking at the questions, she didn't have time, she was just copying exactly what I had written over onto her blank page.

'Sara's a bitch,' she said without looking up. I put the wet towel bundle of shampoo and leave-in conditioner down.

'I know,' I replied.

*

That morning session at the pool, the boys had started a chant that I'd heard them do quietly on the bus before; now, they were emboldened by the fact that they were all in the second group and that it was the first time in the season we were doing a kind of sprint set. Dan turned to one of the other boys, a very fair-haired, very blond boy in my year; another new girl, who had a large nose and whose face was always red, was walking up the far side of the pool. 'Who's that coming over the hill, is it a monster?' he sang. One of the older boys turned, 'Nah, it's Sinead!'

Roan had his back to them, writing the set on the whiteboard; all the boys had fallen about laughing and it looked to me as if he laughed as well. I turned the scene over in my head as I stood outside the corner shop, waiting for Amelia and some of the other girls to buy white chocolate buttons and strawberry laces, watching for the bus and tracing Sinead's face in my mind – the way her eyebrows sloped down naturally, as though she was constantly prepared to be crestfallen – and her chubby hands with shorter fingers than palms, her wide hips and wider thighs. She had just turned fourteen.

I wanted to buy something that made me feel like the kind of person who could say, 'It fucking stinks in here.' My mum was never going to get me Uggs, the it-girls' footwear of choice, and I didn't like them anyway, but I needed an object that made me feel like I was on the inside. I wanted the others to know that I knew I was different, but not that different, that the joke wasn't on me. Later, I stood in the stark Superdry changing rooms, holding a pair of faded blue trackies with a fluorescent '6' in bright pink and an equally bright '7' in fluoro-green just by the pocket. They were £80, and when my mum came to pick me up for Christmas, I would maybe ask her to bring me back and get them. Amelia had bought some new make-up in Boots. She was preppy in a way that I didn't understand but was starting to learn that only specific kinds of girls could be: old hand-me-down cashmere jumpers, Jack Wills pants, hair pulled over to one side. It was innate, not rich, just precious, small-town country. I'd never had the feeling before; I didn't know what I wanted to own, I just wanted to buy things.

Saturday night was the weekend, the only evening of the week that wasn't followed by morning training. And after shopping, before the evening film, the girls would get ready. Ready to go into the common room and see the boys; ready to find a spot on the sofa next to the one they liked, if they were asked. Bras from Ann Summers under thin white vest tops with thinner straps, teal-green showing through the see-through white material. Kayli and Sara were taking pictures. Kayli's brown doe eyes angled up and to the right; she looked away from the camera lens, Sara threw a peace sign. I stood in the doorway of Amelia's and my room, watching them. They looked at the back of the digital camera and laughed, then Kayli held it out again and they pushed their hips out away from one another. I missed my friends, I missed my faraway life – the sand dunes in Hout Bay on a Sunday evening with my family, and being the fastest at barefoot racing on the beach, and the hot air hitting my bones as soon as I stepped onto the tarmac at Nairobi airport. I missed the simplicity of home, of feeling exceptional in a good way, but mostly I missed the now-distant feeling of knowing that the way I was was okay.

V

The skin around my eyes stings red and small green squiggles
of numbers, abbreviations and times-symbols dance on the
whiteboard; the bright overhead lights reflect the writing on
the board and the face of the large pace clock above it onto
the surface of the pool. It is still dark outside. The silicone
swim cap hits the nape of your neck extra hard at 5 a.m. And
my breath hits me anew from the yellow plastic rim of my
water bottle after I pull my swimming cap on, as the acrid taste
of the hot air in my mouth mingles with the lemony salt water
that tastes also of yellow plastic. The skin on my forearms is
grey and cracked; around my lips and in neat circles at the top
of my cheekbones my face flakes off in small scab-shaped pieces
if I put my hand to it, mirroring the outline of my goggles.
The socks I have been wearing since the end of the late session
the night before have baked chlorinated moisture into the warm
spaces between my toes and, faintly, I can make out the sweet,

putrid smell of rot; like a slightly infected ear-piercing, the skin between my toes – wet always – is eating itself.

Only one in five mornings did someone talk on the bus on the way to training. You kept your hoodie up, didn't even take the backpack off your shoulders, feeling the duvet on your still-warm body when twenty-seven minutes after opening your eyes you would be submerged in cold water. 'Wake up!' the water commanded as your feet hit, heavy arms barely together, let alone tensed, as they guided you down into the deep end and the cold robbed you of that just-woken warmth.

'Why am I here?' No answer. There hasn't been an answer for years, but the question still rises softly every morning session; the small child that you still are wants to know. Two seams imprint small, sewn lines of tightly woven elastic thread into my shoulders, mapping a short route down my upper back to strong deltoids. Arms swing forward-back-up-behind. Neck twists 20 degrees and my eyes leave the tiled bottom, chin up and to the right. I create a paddle using the whole surface area from my palm to the crook of my elbow. Pull round, slip, down, catch, back. As my thumb grazes my flank near the open hole of the back of my costume, I feel my rubbery dolphin skin, the slippery film the chlorine makes on the surface of your body. I turn my body on a perfect horizontal axis but only from shoulder to hip – my spine is the spit, and I am the pig. The whole pool is held captive by the sound of our breath, so exaggerated and loud, as though its coming from a blowhole, we are all gasping at once, huge inhales to last the full duration of our arms' slow-motion recovery. I watch my arm, out of the corner of my right eye come all the way overhead, slow slow slow – smack. My hand lazily hits the surface of the water and I lull my head round, making eye contact once more with the tiles on the bottom.

After warm-up we sometimes moved lanes before the main set. On a morning like this, it was a mind-numbing 2 kilometres of slow aerobic torture and then we'd find ourselves together again, standing on the side of the pool, the ridges in the no-slip poolside tiles hard on our not-yet-pruned feet, awake and fizzy with the need to interact. Dan, the beautiful mod-looking Northerner who'd quickly established himself as the leader of our swimming pack, picked up the long silver rod behind the whiteboard as we all chose lanes. Your lane wasn't really a choice, and if you picked wrong you would get moved anyway, but the trick was actually to end up in the lane next to whoever you wanted to talk to, going the same time as them. The black and red hands of the pace clock hit 60–30, top and bottom, then swapped thirty seconds later. One half of the hand was red and the other black and they faced away from each other, always thirty seconds apart, telling us when to go, when to stop, how long to rest for, and embedding their command of time within us until we knew, just by feeling, exactly how much time had passed, and how quickly.

As it ticked round, I remembered when I was first taught to use one. Dan tapped me with the pole as I walked past lane four to get from where I was in lane two to the other side of the pool and the memory faded; he was jousting with Jenkins.

'You're going to impale me,' I said, in a mocking voice. I didn't think about my words, the euphemism. The boys immediately burst out laughing, all of them, 'Yeah, you're alright, I really don't want to *impale* you,' Dan replied. I looked back up at the clock, another thirty seconds had passed, and Roan was still explaining the set.

Roan might have been our coach, but the pace clock was our master. Without mercy it presided over every second of rest, looking only ever at its counterpart on the wall above the pool on the other side. The two pace clocks didn't care that they were sometimes just out, with the one at the deep end leading the other by two seconds, robbing us of precious rest when the set stopped us at the other end. These clocks were our language, and instead of an hour, one lap of its hand was only ever sixty seconds.

We were going to do a length every thirty seconds: that was the turnaround time, sixteen times over and that was called one set. Then, we were going to repeat the whole thing six times. Two and a half kilometres of swimming straight butterfly with a single breath per length. Off thirty seconds means you have around ten seconds' rest each length. It's not an exact science; by the time you get to the third set the pace clocks seem to have sped up and it's more like seven seconds, but you can't let it drop below five. Five seconds isn't enough rest to hold your breath for as long as it takes to fly kick underwater 15 metres down the pool's length. You also can't think about how hard it's going to be, how much it's going to hurt, and you can't think more than one set ahead. You hold back just enough in set one that you can make it through set two. Then, once you get to the middle of set two, you have to work harder to keep going at the same pace; here you pick your battle: would you rather do the hardest work underwater, or on the surface?

There are no heroes in a set like this: it's binary. Either you make the whole set properly, which means you do it 85 per cent by the book and the rest of the time you don't get caught cheating. Or you fall apart: your lungs blow up, you lose the mental game and once you miss one turnaround – as you bargain with the pace clocks to slow the seconds down – it's almost impossible to get back on track. The trick to these endless sets is serenity. A mind of steel made of the softest sand, that can be moved, moulded and blown away. The second thing is to only think about one component of the length at a time. You take a deep breath, but not too deep, and when the red hand hits the ten past, your body tight but supple, let the push take you past the flags, yielding and calm underwater, then start. Short, sharp dolphin kick then two longer ones, then back to short and sharp again. Head squeezed between locked arms. Halfway down the pool, at 12.5 metres, there's always a tile placed horizontal in the line down the centre of your lane: just one odd tile to disrupt this vertical flow, it tells you that you're halfway. Three more strong angulations of the body from hip to toe will take you forward to 15 metres then you sail up, crashing through the surface, head down, hips up, throwing both arms overhead and forwards, always forwards. No breathing on the first stroke. Butterfly looks hard, and it is, all shoulders and stomach. One stroke, then your first breath, finally: you're almost at 20 metres now. The board says '*br ev 3*' – that means you need to take another three strokes with your head down; but the board also says '*no br last 5m*' – that means your last breath is stolen from you because you're already under the flags that signify 5 metres to the wall. And you keep your head down until you touch the wall with two hands, always with two hands for fly, even in training. Okay. One set down.

Fifteen metres underwater. I always picked underwater; I liked the noiseless cocoon, my eyes fixed on the dark-tiled line directly underneath me, guiding my soft, sandy mind to the other side. It's not hard in the first set, it's not even hard in the second set, but by the third, your brain starts to pop and move: starved of oxygen, it feels like parts of it are pushing out of a permeable skull and being shed into the water. You don't panic, but you're not even halfway through; with three sets still to go, you have to go somewhere else. You go somewhere in your mind, not to a beach or the podium, but to small moments of triumph. Tiny little victories, the beautiful scenarios that affirm all the good things you believe about yourself and shut out all the bad. The joke you told in class the other day when everyone laughed; immediately after you got your test back with full marks and you got to sit at the back. And what will the next such scenario be . . . These daydreams help you hold your breath. During 15 metres, I would push to 17: the trade-off was fewer strokes, saving my shoulders and taking a wrecking ball to my lungs instead. If you make it past set three and you're still holding on, then it starts to get easier. This is the swimmer's equivalent of the runner's high. These sets aren't designed to produce lactic acid build-up; they're not even designed to make you faster. The ten precious seconds at each end make it possible; fingers pushed into the small, squishy space under your throat, heart rate drops, 160, 120, 89. But these sets aren't about swimming at all. All the rules and the precious seconds that slip away as you watch the clock, waiting, panting. These sets are designed only to make you tough.

You'll first know you're in trouble when you start to feel your head moving upwards just a millisecond too late. As fatigue draws in, your hips rise and your pelvis tilts towards the wall at the end of the pool. At exactly the same time, your chin should lift 3 or 4 centimetres above the surface to snatch a breath and as you lower your eyes and place your head down into the water, your arms follow after. When you're tired, your arms are nearly at your ears by the time your brain tells your neck 'lift, breathe'. Technique breaks down. You're playing catch-up with the rhythm your body has set for you, and you can't even keep up with yourself. And if you don't breathe every three strokes, you are made to get out and do twenty press-ups. That's getting off lightly. If you don't make the 15 metres underwater, you do extra lengths in the rest between sets, with everyone watching. Worse still, if you're caught more than once in the same set, the whole squad is made to start the set again and everyone knows it's because of you. And the very worst punishment, when you cease to make the turnaround, is when you give up the right to continue the session, in the same way or at all.

By the third round that morning, Sinead's head was barely making it out of the water and her feet were barely making it past the 5-metre flags when she pushed off the wall. Her face was redder than I'd ever seen it. Some of the boys were doing the set with paddles on, large plastic discs that gave you large plastic webbed hands and exist only so the water can pinch the muscles that attach your arms to your body as you drag yourself forward – at least, that's how it felt – making it about 20 per cent harder. After years of doing this same set long course, 50 metres in the freezing-cold pool in South Africa with its broken pump, crying into my goggles at ten years old with my Hungarian coach ordering me to 'swuhm', I didn't exactly find it easy, but I didn't find it hard to do it properly. I had cut my teeth in much less forgiving water than this. Roan intimidated me, but at least the pool was warm. At the end of that set, I watched Roan glance up at the pace clock as Sinead came in two seconds after the turnaround. This is how it happens: you see the weak one in the herd and the embarrassment starts: they become an example of how to fail, how to lose. We knew that we weren't directly in competition with each other, but what we didn't know, not consciously anyway, is that we were always in competition for affection, for attention, for affirmation. To be the best in the pool and have our coach know it too, that's all we wanted; and Roan used that. He used that to push us harder and he used it to make us harder.

'Who wants to take the next set for Sinead?' he asked. 'Because she's not making the turnaround.' Sinead was clinging onto the edge of the wall, just where it met the lane rope, her fingers curled around the small lip under the ledge of the top of the pool. She was wearing a red swimming cap and her whole body was red; mottled across the back of her shoulders were splotches of crimson red and a small heat rash spread in a constellation between her shoulder blades. We were dripping with sweat; we always were but we never felt it in the water. The boys had their bottles above their heads, squeezed and held upside-down so the cold, unchlorinated tap water ran down from their foreheads and cooled their hot faces at the end of the set.

'Anyone?' Roan said again. After a further fifteen seconds, Jenkins put his hand up in the far lane, 'I'll do it, I'll do four,' he said shortly. I was proving myself in this set and I wanted Roan to see that, to see me. 'I'll do some – I'll do some as well,' I said quickly. I looked at Sinead, tried to rearrange my face so that there was no pity in my eyes. 'Thank you,' she mouthed at me, the contortion of pain making her broad face look like a Roald Dahl character, the humiliation more painful to her than the set itself.

'Okay, thirty seconds, on the red top,' Roan started, adding, 'And lucky Sinead only has to do eight.'

*

Life changed immeasurably that first term, sometimes even day to day, but it was all held in the frame of the sessions that made up the cycle of our weekly training. The weeks were seasonal in their sameness. And not only did this mean that we had a strange relationship with time, but also that it was easy to overlook and underestimate the gravity of the things that were happening to and around us, and sometimes also by us. The structure brought a heightened rhythm to our life and like the black and red hands of the pace clock, changing places every thirty seconds, it was hard for outsiders to understand. Each moment of it was so specific and acute that it started to become comfortable, then comforting; and, much like being in prison, after a while we didn't want anything different. We didn't want Tuesday evening's late session not to be followed by a 4.45 a.m. wake-up and we didn't want the heavy-legs session in the gym not to be followed by a sprint set the next afternoon, when we could barely move from the waist down and getting out of bed we'd feel tiny tears in the tender muscles we'd already shredded, like ripping an already crumpled piece of paper again and again and again.

The set plan for the week made our life make sense; it made the bizarre sacrifices quantifiable. Just get through the next session. However painful, it made us feel safe, the comfort and familiarity of our routine. It was the only thing that made the training possible. That everything could be divided up into blocks of time and blocks of work and blocks of weeks. And blocks of sessions. Blocks of hours, blocks of minutes. Blocks of seconds, blocks of milliseconds. Time was divisible to 00.01. It was what it took to win, and it was what it cost to lose. And whether you won or lost, the weeks kept happening again and again, always the same. Monday morning threshold, Monday evening aerobic. Tuesday evening sprint. Wednesday morning drills. Wednesday evening aerobic followed by weights. Thursday evening sprint session again. Friday morning aerobic, Friday evening recovery, then run. Saturday morning sprint, then weights again. Sunday rest and wait to repeat.

VI

'I'll tell you what men are like,' Kayli said, tucking her hair behind her ear. 'At Christmas last year we had friends over for drinks, and one of my dad's friends, who said his family was ill at home, spent all night talking to me about politics and schools and my ideas about how children should be raised; he talked to me like I was an adult. At the end of the party, he didn't know how to get to the bottom of the estate, so I walked him down, and after all night talking about his kids and his wife back at home, we got to the taxi and he said, "So how do we do this then?" and I said, "Do what?" and then he tried to kiss me. And that's what men are like.'

'You need to not move for a second.' I held the needle tightly. 'Will you tell me when you're going to do it?' 'No,' I replied. We both fell quiet, and I returned to her story, considering this man getting close enough, as I was, to see the tiny honey-blonde hairs on her cheek catching the light down to her jawline. 'Don't you think it's kind of ridiculous that we have to do the early set again tomorrow?' She broke our silence, and in response I touched the tip of the needle to the softest part of her velvet earlobe and without hesitating pushed down hard. I felt it push through the skin, felt her tense her shoulders and her back arch, felt the needle slow down as it hit the thin layer of cartilage and heard the tiny pop as it appeared out the other side. 'No,' I said, 'I think it's kind of ridiculous that we have to train on Saturday morning, then get straight on a bus and compete at Devon County Championships all weekend.'

I had long believed, and subsequently understood, that adults never really grew up. So it seemed impossible that they could have appropriate relationships with children anyway. But I wondered whether this precluded them from trying. Whether they were supposed to try to create distance, because they were allowed to tell you what to do. Roan and Julia, our two main coaches, were very different. I felt Roan was bullish, conceited, all ego. Julia was process-oriented, form-obsessed, and sometimes it felt like she wanted to possess us. She was the breaststroke coach and we worshipped her, we would swim for her, push another hard session for her; she was kind and funny, but brutal, and she never let up. In one of my early sessions we were pushing hard drills, something called an eggbeater kick, like a strange alternating frog leg: each leg kicking out strong from the hip in a one-legged breaststroke style, body bolt upright, shoulders above the water while your legs were working fiercely under the surface to keep you up. We did this to build strong quads; breaststroke is all in the leg strength, and under Julia, my quads swelled. Eggbeater kick with a 5-kilogram rubberised brick clutched to your chest: thirty seconds at chest, thirty seconds holding it up at eye level, thirty seconds holding it above the head with arms locked out straight, then thirty seconds rest, then again and again. I was the best, better than most of the boys, and in these breaststroke-only sessions Julia would be frenzied; she loved how specialised my body seemed, how innate it all was for me. Sometimes the girls would do twenty seconds instead of thirty, but she would push me on, 'Come on, Chay,' she'd call, 'come on, stay up with the boys.'

In the fifth round, my knee popped out of its socket. The image of a baseball bat and an exploding watermelon hung in my mind just long enough for a bolt of electricity to shoot down the inside of my thigh, and as the brick slipped out of my hand and my garbled scream was subsumed by the water, my ears slipped under the surface just long enough for me to hear it. A dull, localised sound. It made me gag; jacket potato, beans and cheese, lunch that felt so long ago, reintroduced themselves to me as I heard my knee exit its socket like taking two handfuls of matted hair and tearing them apart while also tearing them from someone's head. Then the pop. As my kneecap travelled up towards my thigh I travelled back up to the surface. Gasping, I heaved myself onto the side of the pool. I couldn't walk so I crawled, not knowing if anyone was watching because I couldn't see. I pulled myself up onto a large step by the side of the pool. Julia glanced back at me but she was still running the set and assumed, as would anyone, that I had cramp; she was a physio by trade, before she became a coach, and she still practised; if she knew what had happened to my knee I might be out for weeks. I grabbed at the foam kick board next to me and placed it under my head, then pushed my back and shoulders into the hard tiles, almost trying to transfer the pain. My heart rate started to drop, and I wrenched my eyes open to inspect the damage. I'd seen someone do it before, not to themselves, but I assumed it would be just the same. I brought my left hand down onto the bottom of my thigh, and lifted the top of my body up to a sitting position so I could apply the downward pressure that would push my roaming kneecap back into place. I closed my eyes once more and exhaled. Then put my hands to my forehead. Just as I felt my body relax I snapped my eyes open, pushed my leg into the wall at the end of the step, twisted it to the left and pushed down, hard. I thought I would scream but I was so shocked I didn't make a sound, then I quickly swung both legs round and put some weight on my feet as I faced the pool. The session had continued as normal; no one had noticed. Julia looked back at me again, her dark auburn hair slightly inflated because of the heat rising from the chlorinated water, the charcoal eyeliner on her top lids slightly faded. 'Get back in,' she said.

Julia was also my friend – unlike Roan. My memory of him is of a man who might laugh with some of the boys but ultimately saw us as prizewinners; it was as if we were pageant children, all dressed up in bright royal blue and road-line yellow everything: swimming caps, costumes, polos, bottles. They did things differently; they each wanted something different out of it, but because of the system they operated in they both wanted to control our bodies, our youth a vehicle for their own ambitions. Roan wanted to build the best club in the country so that he could say that it was his – at least, that's what I naively thought at the beginning – and Julia wanted to achieve technical greatness, the kind of perfection that comes along once in a generation: the perfect race. I wanted to be the best and I also wanted to win, and I was starting to realise that those were different things. Roan and Julia knew this, although neither acknowledged that the other was in pursuit of the opposite. To be the best one had to surrender, and to win one had to withstand. The better I got, the more I was locked in a battle of yielding and resisting, Roan wanted me tough and mean, Julia wanted me supple and smart, but both of them wanted me, and I knew I would eventually have to choose.

If you let it, swimming allows you to know more and more about yourself. The sheer amount of time spent alone leads you to observe yourself frequently, especially in the long, lonely aerobic mornings where you swim up to 8 kilometres a session. Instead of counting tiles on the bottom of the pool, you start to fill in the gaps of your memories, building complete pictures of times gone by to re-experience the feelings you felt then, but with more richness now in the silence of the water. The depth of these reflections turns into new ways of knowing and, for me, also an anxious paranoia, as I turned these thoughts over and over on a multidimensional plane and built them from every angle with all these laps of the pool, and hours and hours alone, in the water.

I knew that I got nervous in a different way to other people. A kind of focus that started with my eyes: strong, unmoving. An energy that radiated from them and held my cheeks taut and the muscles in my jaw not clenched, not soft, just set. The focus created a kind of forcefield around me: I used it to incite fear, to intimidate, to throw people off their game before the race had begun. As I got better, I learned how to wield it to deepen others' nerves, how to use it to be chatty and casual in the call room, the twenty-minute holding pen you sat in with your competitors before walking out for your race. The call room was a tomb of anxiety that held thirty-two nervous swimmers at a time, the next four races lined up in plastic chairs in qual-ifying order, the fastest in the middle, lane four, then alternating out to the ends: the second- and third-fastest qualifiers get lanes five then three, then six and two, then seven and one, then the slowest in lane eight. More often than not, the water in the pool creates an arrowhead and the waves created by the fastest swimmers in the middle wash out to the sides, hit against them, and then the slower swimmers must battle the waves again as they bounce off the walls and back into their outside lanes. I used the weight of my forcefield against my competitors, seeming nonchalant about my training and preparation – 'Oh, I've been so ill for the last couple of weeks,' I'd say, 'Yeah, whatever, I can't even believe my coach is making me do this' – all the while being ranked first into the final, three seconds clear of anyone else. And in swimming, three seconds is an eternity.

The first time, it was only a county competition, but I had to start winning somewhere, and at the beginning I liked the small stage. I liked the power and the practice; I liked the space between heats and finals. On the morning of the competition, you swam sloppy and unconcentrated in the heats, but even then, some people would put full racing costumes on. As part of my performance, I started to always swim heats in a normal swimming costume: I liked to beat people without the tools, creating a mythology. And then in the evening, when we came back for finals, as the calculator-like letters and numbers flashed up on the scoreboards that looked like a live train departure board I would sometimes pretend we were at a much bigger competition: World Short Course Championships, with an American to my right and a Russian to my left. We'd sit in the call room, and I'd wait until the very last minute to take off all my clothes behind the starting block. Walking down the pool length, all in a row, we'd filter behind the lanes to my favourite sound, the enduring sound of my career, 'And in lane four,' the commentator would start in a voice like a circus ringmaster, 'from Plymouth Leander,' – or Team GB, as I'd say in my head, dreaming of my future on the world stage – 'ranked first into the final, with a time of 57.63, we have Achieng Ajulu-Bushell.' And people would cheer, and everyone would already know that I was going to win.

We all got changed on poolside after training at school that Saturday morning; because we were going to be back in a pool to warm up for the heat's session of the weekend-long competition in less than an hour, there didn't seem any point in getting dressed properly. County Championships were treated like an extension of training. As we started to develop our technique, we began to practise racing in our weekly sessions, getting ready for the bigger competitions later that summer. Countys were the perfect mechanism, a low-stakes event that went on for four weekends in January. Each weekend we would train early on a Saturday morning, a gruelling sprint set, and then get changed and on the bus to drive the hour to a public pool somewhere in Devon, to compete all weekend. There and back on Saturday, and there and back on a Sunday.

On the coach Jenkins was talking to Dan as always; he had a soft accent, and I knew he was from a place that wasn't a big city. His torso was long, and it would have looked stupid if his shoulders weren't almost as wide; he was backlit in front of the big windows and soft winter light made the small water drop-lets glow as they fell from his hair, which would later dry in large ringlets. Unfocused, I had to retie my shoelaces and I caught Kayli's eye as I bent to try again. She smiled at me knowingly: maybe about Jenkins, or maybe we were friends now after I had pierced her ear in the boarding house the night before.

Sport, like the arena of adolescence, is a hyper-gendered space. And the combination of the two was potent. The girls fought to be the most girl, and the boys to be the most boy. The most boy was the fastest, strongest, loudest, gruffest, the one who got the most action and the most laughs. The most girl was the prettiest, coolest, sexiest, 'I can get down with the guys', demure, unmanly, no visible muscles, not too fast, not too impressive, not too much wanting to win, long hair on her head and none on the rest of her body, make-up, and trackies rolled down at the hips with the tip of a lace thong showing.

In the final of the thirteen-year-old 100-metre freestyle I swam under fifty-eight seconds. I looked up at the scoreboard and saw Kayli sitting in the gallery just above it. The Girls 16-year-old 100-metre freestyle final had been last weekend. I wasn't a freestyle swimmer like Kayli, and I wasn't even supposed to be considered a sprinter yet – I was still too young to specialise – but I had just swum faster than her. I knew she saw my faint self-conscious smile as I looked up at her, but she turned her head and behind a hand she whispered something to Sara, who tapped another one of the older girls to her right, who leaned in to listen. On the bus on the way back to the boarding house that evening I sat alone. There was one small pull-out seat in the middle of the minibus that folded down so that people could get to the three rows at the back. I knew Roan was happy with me and that Julia was indifferent. I lay against the cold glass of the window and let the vehicle vibrate against my forehead, matching the faraway snuffle of the rest of the team asleep. I could hear giggling in the back, and in front of me Jenkins' curls lay carefully between the headrest and the top of the seat. The team captain, a Scottish boy in upper sixth with hair just like a man across his chest and torso, had his arm around one of the older girls, pulling her close as his other hand moved down to her hips. I turned away quickly and could hear the elastic stretch as he put it into her trackies.

VII

This was to be my last year at the South African Nationals. I didn't know how much things were about to change, and I still had the unbridled energy of my early youth to carry me through competition after competition, sometimes swimming more than twenty races in a week. In Kenya after school, my mum would make obstacle courses outside. She'd sit at the top of our long sprawling garden timing me as I did star jumps and cartwheels, army-crawled down the sloping lawn, then ran down to the trampoline to perform four front flips before jumping off, running round a tree and picking up the prize she had left for me, a frisbee, or a small juggling ball, then sprinting headlong up the garden again. I would do this until I couldn't see my hands in front of me, until the 7 p.m. shadows crept to the veranda and finally, not exhausted, but tired, I'd go inside. I'd been training my body for this kind of exertion long before there was a place on a podium at stake. Overhead, the weather hung close: not East African sun, just a bright grey sky that felt like it was pinned to the top of the arena. The blocks were built of concrete, unmoving and ungiving. It was as if the whole pool had been carved out of the earth, just sprang up halfway between Cape Town and Durban. An artefact of apartheid horror in a small town on the Indian Ocean called East London. Hard concrete bricks surrounded the water, and even though I couldn't feel the sun shining, it burned my feet in the middle of the day when I walked from the grassy bank around the left side of the pool, where all the club tents were set up, to the stands.

Because I was competing internationally for Kenya, my mum encouraged me to go back to South Africa for their Age Group Championships: a chance to see my friends, to be back in a space where I wasn't the only one who looked like me. And a chance to compete on African soil. The times that I had set back in the UK qualified me for international competition as part of the Kenyan team; you can qualify at any FINA-certified meet. But somehow she thought that this was important, and these Level 3 Nationals fell just before my birthday in March, so I got to compete at the top of my age group too. Old friends also meant old rivals: a short, very strong, stocky girl with strange technique, Megan, had been my main competition when I'd left South Africa not even a year ago. She'd peaked early, her body developed forward from her chest, not in breasts but in mass, like she was growing in the wrong direction, which wasn't uncommon for girls but for a time it did make her seem exceptional, unbeatable, with no end to her times coming down and down and down. Broad-shouldered, she was becoming a breaststroke swimmer like me. Her head jerked slightly to the right when she broke the surface of the water and pulled back, her chin meeting her neck before she pushed it down again. Everyone remarked on her technique, this strange idiosyncrasy. Anything different is always seen as an advantage when you're winning, and as soon as you're not it's seen as your fault.

I came back from these Nationals with thirteen gold medals; I won every single event that I'd entered. It was a turning point. The year before there had been a smattering of some silver and one bronze and there were fewer in the bunch. The year before that, I only had six medals, and none of them gold either. The hardest thing about that week was how easily I beat Megan. I won again and again, and I watched her crumble, frustrated, unable to explain to herself or anyone else how or why it was happening. She wasn't swimming any slower than before; I was just suddenly faster, quicker off the block, confident into the turns, stronger down the last length. We were only thirteen years old, but we were learning the oldest lesson that competitive sport had to teach: being outperformed is as inevitable as breathing, and when it first happens to you, it always feels inexplicable.

'You think I don't know you're unfocused? You'd better fix this, Meg.' He was holding her by her bicep and I could see his thumb slightly digging into a dappled patch of her suntanned skin. She stared back at him blankly, her face still hot from our race. 'You think anyone wants to watch you swim like this?' He was getting louder. 'Are you going to answer me or are you going to let that Black girl keep beating you?' I hadn't heard anyone approach as I watched the man continue to hold her tightly by the arm and listened to him talk to her, or at her, about me. But suddenly I felt breath on my neck. A hurried whisper: 'Everyone knows he's completely insane, come on!' It was a girl from my old club in Cape Town, a blonde Afrikaans girl with icy grey eyes that sloped down at the corners. She looped her arm through mine and pulled me away from my vantage point. 'After you left last year,' she went on as we walked away, 'Meg almost qualified for the Games. It was completely crazy, she was so young, shame, it was so awful, and you know that club is also completely mad, they train like they're in war camp.' She paused. 'But then, when she didn't make the qualifying time, I don't know, it just seemed even more messed up.'

In the silence of the call room, I could hear the sound of fingers twitching, tapping on the cool metal where our plastic chairs touched. Megan was sitting next to me swinging her bare feet back and forth; they weren't even close to touching the ground. A cheap white headphone cable dangled between us; our heads tilted slightly towards each other. The song was skittish and high-pitched, and I had to block it out to hear Megan talking because we had headphones in the ears closest to each other. 'It all just happened so fast, and now we're here again, I feel like we've been coming here forever,' Megan said. 'I know,' I replied. 'It's weird, even though it's always in a different place it also feels the same, it feels more the same every year – you know?' We let the question hang between us. 'Yah,' Megan started. 'I mean – it's not . . . what

I thought it was going to be like.' The music surged, we both sang along and pushed our hands out to the same side and changed them in time to the beat. 'So,' I looked at her, 'shall we go out hard?' – 'I don't know man, I'm so tired.' Her head hung down slightly as she responded, shame mixed with defeat. – 'Come on, it's only day two,' I said. I studied her face; she seemed so small in the grainy plastic chair, with her upturned nose and a soft line on her forehead from her swimming cap and constantly training outdoors. 'I'm so tired since last season,' she said at last. – 'Well, look, you're always faster on the back-end than me anyway,' I tried to console her. – 'Yeah, but my legs feel so heavy.' – 'Okay, I'll lead; you know we've got the 100-metre final in an hour too.' – 'If you lead out fast, maybe we'll go under 2.30.' She started laughing as she said it. – 'Yeah, right, you have no idea how much the altitude is killing me,' I retorted. – 'We're not even at altitude.' She was laughing still. – 'I know,' I smiled at her, 'I've just gotten so used to saying that when people back in the UK ask about competitions here; they have no idea.' – 'What's it like?' she asked. I wasn't sure she cared. – 'I don't know, it's weird, there are, like, no parents around, ever.' We went silent; we were the only ones still talking and we were about to walk out. – 'Okay, good luck,' she said. I was reaching down to pull the legs of my costume up so the material sat better around my pelvis, slowly coaxing it with my fingers like a pair of tights. Megan squeezed my shoulder and stood up to flip her long, pale hair forward, fried and light at the ends from chlorine and sun damage; as she stuffed it into the back of her swimming cap, she caught the headphone wire and the earbuds fell out of our ears and onto the ground.

On the flight back to Heathrow I stayed awake until I knew we were close to Kenya. The pilot announced this by telling us that the peak of Kilimanjaro was visible above the clouds on our left, and as they parted I saw the landscape of my homeland below. I loved the strange square bodies of water and the small low-hanging clouds, lonely mist that had wandered too far from its clan. The hills looked like peace. I breathed in the muddy green view and let small, homeless tears run slowly down my cheeks. I closed my eyes and thought of my mother's smell: vetiver, sweet melon, sandalwood, and her soft voice as she rubbed my temples, 'It's okay, baby bear,' she'd say to me. 'Everything's going to be okay.' At the airport, before I boarded the flight to leave Johannesburg, I was supposed to see my father. I waited, pacing and watching the flights board. I called him – and then called again. He was always coming, he told me: 'I'm almost there, baby girl, don't be like that.' In the end I went through security and called him a last time, venomous. 'You always do this, you're always late and you don't care about me, you don't think about me, I'm always waiting for you.' When I was sitting at the gate, waiting, a small, hunched security guard came over. He was holding a stiff cream card bag with black-and-white striped tissue paper, crunched and sticking out from the top. 'Are you the daughter of the professor?' he asked me loudly. – 'Yes,' I answered back in a tone that I hoped would lower his. – 'Your father left this for you.' He handed me the bag and shuffled away. It seemed as though the blue felt chair tilted backwards as I took the bag from him, and I wanted the chair to snap shut and swallow me. 'Happy Belated Birthday!' the note read. It wasn't my birthday yet. Inside was a small box, round, deep and beautiful, a mirror to my eyes; it held two diamond earrings set in generous silver clasps. I knew they were real because of the weight of them and noted the tiny stamp on the side of the silver. I took out the phone he had bought me the year before: no battery. I walked slowly to the pay phone just between my gate and the next. After the coins fell, I dialled his number and waited the full thirty-eight seconds until the receiver hung up on me.

*

The blocks were white fibreglass down the side with a gritty royal-blue lining on their surface and a tilted block that locked into place on five different settings. There was a diving pool which doubled as a swim-down pool and the floor of the main pool went up and down electronically so it could be 25 or 50 metres long. Ten glittering lanes with anti-wave lane ropes and stands up each side. Ponds Forge International Sports Centre. Soon, we wouldn't know anything else, and even though I was aiming beyond it, there was something about this pool in Sheffield, an energy, maybe because this was the top of many people's swimming career, the site of a thousand victories and a thousand more failures; the home of National Championships and Olympic Qualifiers. All the most important national competitions of the country were swum here. And the very first time I saw it was in my first season with the club, in March 2008, for the National Speedo Swimming League.

Roan pulled me aside after warm-up; even when he sat on the makeshift metal stands on poolside his eyes were level with mine. I could feel my teammates' jealous eyes on me, feel their intrigue. He was larger than life, his head became his neck without tapering, his hand enveloped my whole head as he pulled me closer to him.

'I need you to do this for the squad,' he started. 'I know you're tired, but we have a chance here, if you swim up, we have a real chance and we only have to win half of the relays to stay ahead. It's going to be eight races in one afternoon, can you do it for me? For the squad?' I knew he could smell my fear as I nodded. You can't make a good swim out of fear or sadness – you can be nervous, but it has to come from euphoria, belief and a lack of self-consciousness. A performance personality you've developed that is distinct from your own. The kind of person who will take the mic at a karaoke if that's what they're most scared of. For me, it was far simpler. I was scared to fail so sometimes I held back, took myself out of the running before the race had even started. But in order to get to the next level, I had to face that fear down. 'No guts, no glory,' Roan would say over and over. No guts, no glory.

I was 5 foot 3 and weighed less than 50 kilos; my little finger was twitching uncontrollably from a mixture of exhaustion and lactic acid. I held my hand still by my side. Roan looked across at me and nodded. I had just swum the Girls 13-and-under and then the 15-and-under 100-metre breaststroke back-to-back. My

71

heart rate was still over 120, and I was about to walk back down the pool to swim the Girls 17-and-under too. I wasn't going to win, my body was too exhausted, but I would post more points by touching in the top three than anyone else in my club. The National Speedo League is an annual competition, where the ten best clubs in the country compete for the top honours, a complex point-scoring system and a combination of individual swims and relays. For the first time in our club's history, we were going to win. I put my shoulders back, chin up, goggles on to hide my trembling eyelids.

'Let's get her going.' Roan turned to the team. 'Who are we? Blue army. Who are we? Blue army.' Dan was screaming now; I could hear his voice above the rest as the chant filled the stadium. 'Who are we? Blue army. Who are we? Blue army.' I would have done anything for them then. I would have swum till I drowned.

VIII

The boarding house felt stale and restless. It was almost the end of term, and we couldn't stand each other for much longer. I had been texting Jenkins for the last couple of weeks, savouring each message and passing time aimlessly between each of his slow, one-line replies. Amid the distraction of boys, relentless training and end-of-year exams, the term had disappeared quickly and without drama, until Amelia – my roommate and closest friend – stopped talking to me. I didn't know if it was because we were both breaststrokers and the punishment of competing against each other, sharing a room and my constant improving was getting to be too much. But she also had a boyfriend, unlike me, and recently all the common-room chatter had turned to sex. It created the kind of divide that only teenage girls can understand. She sat self-consciously on the edge of these conversations, but I wasn't invited to join in at all, and so it never occurred to me that she might not want to be in them either.

A couple of weeks earlier, the boys had started spreading rumours about who was having sex in the boarding house. Another of the girls became their favourite topic after the boy she'd supposedly slept with told almost all of them within hours. Sara and some of the other older girls, Kat, a girl with large teeth, and another girl called Abi, had pulled together in response – that's how the exclusive club first formed – and they seemed to be plotting, enveloping the girl and comforting each other. Even on the outside, in quiet reflection, I couldn't seem to muster an emotional response to how the girl must be feeling, I could only think about the fact that I was nowhere near having sex. Everyone talked about it for weeks, all the way to the end of term, until everyone knew, mock teasing her: on the bus on the way to training and on the bus on the way back from weights, on poolside, in the queue on the way to breakfast and walking in a pack on the way to training again. Nothing happened, no adult intervention, nothing; and so it became a non-event despite feeling so seismic, then the conversation changed and so did our sense of what was okay.

We had one more short course competition left that season and I was desperate to get my time under one minute ten. In every stroke, in every distance, there's a specific time threshold, which, if you puncture it, you pass over into the land of the *real* swimmers. In 100-metre breaststroke that time was one minute and ten seconds. Swim under 1.10.00 and you were on the other side of a forcefield: somewhere different, a league away from the rest of the pack. 'I think you're ready,' Roan had told me one session, and I couldn't let it go. The idea that I could go under 1.10.00 was intoxicating. There were only maybe two people in the country swimming under 1.10.00 then, and certainly none my age. The best way to do it was to first try short course: in a 25-metre pool you have more walls, which means more push-offs, which means faster times. And that weekend, I told myself, I was going to break the threshold.

Before we left for the competition in Hazlemere, I had one more morning training session to get through, and also a Friday night in the boarding house. The evening before a weekend-long competition, at least any proper competitions, we didn't train; you needed a session's rest so you didn't have heavy legs. In order to speed up that process of rest, we would lie on our backs in the common-room, scantily clad in pyjama shorts, with the boys; and with our bums up against the skirting boards we would put our legs up against the wall to flush all the blood from our tired quads to stop it pooling and to calm our nervous systems. Jenkins was lying next to me in just his baggy gym shorts, which gravity had pushed up against the top of his thighs and the defined lattice of muscles, almost in a plait down the front of his leg, was visible up to his hip flexors, where the hair became coarser and his tan started to fade to a milky white. I dug my fingers into the carpet near his back. He was only a couple of years older than me but already well over 6 foot. He had his left hand behind his head, his biceps flexed without thinking, and I could hear the sound of his rough fingers rubbing against the sandy brown curls in his hair. With his right hand he held his phone up to his face and I tried to look out of the corner of my eye to see if he was messaging this girl at Portsmouth that everyone had told me he liked. Exasperated, I turned my head towards him and put my cheek onto the rough green carpet to study the freckles around the bottom of his armpit. His right thumb moved slowly across the keypad of his phone, too big for the tiny buttons as they clacked in time to our breathing. He exhaled loudly, suddenly; and without looking at me he took his hand from behind his head and put his arm down in the space between us and laced his fingers around mine. Paralysed, I held my breath as he put his phone down on his bare chest and turned his face towards mine. I saw the smile in his eyes before I realised that it was for me, the freckled skin creasing around his too-long eyelashes and the amber flecks tightening in his green eyes as they narrowed in a friendly way. 'I was just texting my sister,' he said. His fingers moved to the inside of my wrist and he stroked softly down to my palm. 'I have to go,' he finished, and left me alone on the scratchy floor.

*

'You need to go and speak to Roan about what big competitions you're going to do next year, because I called him and told him that Kenyan Swimming want you to go to the World Championships, but it might be the same time as the British Nationals.' Mum paused to say something to my sister, who was sitting in the car beside her far away in Nairobi, where she was calling from. 'Anyway,' she went on, 'I've also emailed Amelia's mum and the boarding house to give permission for you to stay with them after Hazlemere, and from there you can go down to Brighton and stay with Paul and he will take you to Heathrow and then we'll see you at the beginning of August, okay? Love you, okay, I love you, bye, girls say bye too,' and the voicemail was over. I took my phone away from my ear and carried on packing. Paul would still take me into his family over the holidays. I loved going down there less and less because I hated leaving them, and because I knew that one day I would be too old to need someone to take me to the airport, and maybe that was the only reason he still let me stay.

On poolside after our race, Julia was talking to Lucy and Amelia; they'd been in lanes six and eight in my final. As I waited my turn to review my splits, I pulled at the shammy towel in my bag. The spongy rayon material, like carpet insulator or relaxed hair, held ten times its weight in water. I hadn't noticed that Kayli had been studying me even though she was sitting just to the right of my bag and when I finally looked up, I was taken aback by the look on her face. Contorted in a horrible sarcastic twist, the corners of her mouth turned down and her doe eyes were hard and almost beady.

'If you keep doing things like that, you won't have any friends,' she spat almost silently. It landed hard on my chest like real hatred, and I knew what she was talking about straight away. When I'd finished my race, just moments before, I'd looked up at the score board and let my anger betray me for a split second. I'd snatched my goggles from my head and smashed them hard into the water with my fist clenched around the strap while letting out a groan of frustration, loud enough for people to hear. Other swimmers did it too, only not when

77

they won, which I had, and when no one else in the pool had even finished the race yet. I looked at Kayli silently and held her gaze for a second longer than was comfortable, then turned back around and took my swimming cap off. I finished getting my splits, the breakdown of my time each length, how long it took me to get to 15 metres, and told Julia how many strokes I'd done each length. Roan didn't look at me. Julia clapped her palms flat around my cheeks. 'It's fine, it's fine, we'll get it next season,' she sang. 1.10.56. After Kayli had busied herself talking to someone else about what she was going to wear at the weekend and I knew she wasn't looking, I walked slowly to the changing rooms. I chose a stall at the end of the furthest row back on the left, locked the door, sat on the ledge and cried until I didn't have any more tears; red hot, they burned my cheeks, which were already flushed with chlorine and frustration. I wanted to be a faster swimmer and I really wanted to be liked, and today I was neither.

Still in my costume and still wet from the damp in the changing rooms and my sodden shammy around my neck the commentator's voice rang out around the pool. I walked the catwalk, as we called it, past my team at the far end of the pool and also past everyone else. A short mixed-race girl from a Welsh club, with a beautiful, arresting face and chestnut hair the same colour as her skin, like mine, smiled wide at me.

'Chay!' she shouted as I walked past. – 'I have to go up quickly, but I'll find you after.' I inclined my head in the direction of the podium at the top of the pool. – 'Let's catch up in the showers!' She smiled wider still. We barely knew each other but I loved her, and I knew she loved me too; a safety we had never known we found in each other's presence on the rare occasions that our clubs swam at the same meet. I knew people now, friends almost, but not close enough to stop me from feeling alone. I saw a boy from a London club as I walked up further, 'Bruv,' he nodded down at me as I walked past. In the stand behind him the girl that Jenkins liked from Portsmouth was standing with the green ribbon of a bronze medal around her neck, the medallion hanging taut against her chest.

I could see Amelia talking to Sara at the entrance to the pool near where I'd been getting changed. I was ready to leave with her and I had seen her mum get up and leave the stands some five minutes earlier. I knew she could feel me there, holding onto my bag straps with both hands, but they both pretended I wasn't around. 'Just get through it.' I caught the odd sequence of words from their conversation. I knew Amelia wanted to be on the inside, and I knew Sara was the gatekeeper and that I was stuck. My feet stuck to the wet floor and my skin stuck to me.

One of my biggest fears had always been that I would live my whole life across the lake from girls like them: separated from my heritage by my education and my whiteness, separated from Amelia by a melanated membrane that I couldn't rub off. When I was six years old, back in Kenya, I came home from my first competition and spent two hours locked in creation with my wax crayons. A small brown girl with a red band around her neck, the outline of a dark blue swimming costume and a gold medal as big as her head sat untethered in the middle of the page. 'Look, Mum,' I said. 'This is me when I win the Olympics.' I had grown into the waxy crayon girl in the picture. Standing on the podium in Hazlemere, almost nine years later. I looked down at the bright red ribbon that hung around my neck and the water from my costume seeping into the fabric making dark crimson Rorschach splodges across it and the gold medal below, my bare feet on the raised wooden slab, number one, my face still hot from crying. No, this was not at all what I'd thought the journey would feel like.

*

Swimming had become like a video game, a heroin addiction – my neurons firing anew as if with every race I was experiencing the same aesthetic pleasure and on land there was nothing for me. It dulled down the rest of my life; the adrenaline of racing had made me obsessed with the idea of doing it repeatedly, to the point that I didn't believe I could want or need anything else. And although it felt like this had turned down the volume on every other part of my existence, I could still hear their conspiratorial whispers reminding me that, on land, life was still happening, and I wasn't a part of it.

I had made it through my first year, and like the journey to the centre of the earth, I'd journeyed to the centre of myself, the darkest parts. Through the months of solitude, I swam deeper. I reached the mouth of the cave of the next part of me and as I entered there was another up ahead. The light receded behind me, and as I developed a taste for others' defeat my mind grew quiet from fear. I learned that there was nothing I believed in enough, no line I wouldn't cross for myself. I was only me. Treading water in the deepest parts of my mind. I existed as a parallel line to my own life, a dispassionate distance that I couldn't cross; inhabiting the most strategic parts of my brain, I observed myself with detachment. As the term drew to a close and the summer beyond it, I taught myself not to cry. Beyond tears, I found futility – somehow, that brought me a strength I'd never known before. The resolve came from a will to know the worst parts of my being. I entertained all of my cruelty and self-pity, seated at a table; red pigments of my imagination morphed into characters and there I sat with all the Disney villains, the monsters from my childhood and shapeless shadows of past self-loathing. In conversation at this dinner party of my self-worth I broke myself down, retreated from embarrassment, locked shame in a cupboard under the stairs. Dogged in the pursuit of the purest form of myself, a self I was creating for a single purpose. To win. Weightless, shedding all the things that held me back. Lighter than I'd ever been. Shaving all the hair and peach fuzz from my body, just like the day before a big competition; but this time from within. I took a razor to the inside of my head, cutting away at my insecurity with long, clean strokes.

Intensify

IX

'Of unreflecting love – then on the shore
Of the wide world I stand alone, and think
Till love and fame to nothingness do sink.'
John Keats

Underwater the silence becomes quiet. I'd loved this fact my whole life. Lying on my back, a crucifix in the water, I moved my legs slowly to create the slightest flutter in my toes. This was my response to the currents moving beneath me. They told me wordlessly, 'We will transport you,' and my feet responded, 'I will remain still.' The rest of my body was afforded this freedom, stillness, because my feet moved slowly in contract with the movement of the sea. I moved with the water, I always had. I knew how it wanted me to be and I knew how to be that way. I was born on World Water Day, March 22nd, and in Kenya, in small press pieces, they called me the Aqua Ace.

The water slipped over my shoulders and the wind whipped it through my eyelashes. I let the back of my head touch the top of my neck, the vertebrae folding over each other, so my eyes saw the bright blue of the sky behind me and beyond that the coastland. My breath shook and vibrated through my nose, a mixture of salt and freezing-cold water. Inhale. I moved my fingers, splayed out beside me, my arms stroking the water. I could stroke the surface down a line of movement in the water, then angle my wrist slightly and cut down, slipping through to the next layer. Water was like this: thin, imperceptible layers which had different weights. They flowed in different ways, at different speeds, at different temperatures: sometimes it was smooth, fast, new, fresh, or used and spinning in the wrong direction. I loved intensely this relationship of nuanced imagination; it was how I understood my watery home, how we'd always understood each other. I closed my eyes and prepared to blow out through my nose and at the same time I dropped my hips and pulled my arms up against the water in prayer, allowing the resistance to take me down, spinning in the freezing cold. I tried to lose my body, but it was no use; as I slipped and twisted under the choppy waves with my eyelids squeezed together tightly and the salt seeping in I knew, as my body always did in the water, exactly where it was, and which way was up. I broke the surface just in time to hear a girl's piercing scream as she fell from the top board of the diving block into the sea a couple of metres away from me.

Cascading rocks cut away like steps down to the water and a small, man-made plunge pool was dug into a flat area just to the side of the real concrete steps that fed all the way down into the sea and a metal handrail that disappeared below the surface with them. Jutting out into the water was an old landmark of Plymouth Hoe, four boards built like a professional diving block, the lowest at 6 metres, the highest a terrifying 18. They had been boarded up with mesh grates around the entrance steps and locked to the metal frame of the block, but the locks had been broken and the mesh peeled back and every summer kids climbed up to the top and, sometimes three at a time, jumped into the Atlantic Ocean. I don't know how we knew about this place; no one had time to go out, which meant we rarely spent time with anyone that was not each other, but we all had to be back in Plymouth for pre-season by the end of the third week of August, a full two weeks before term started. And although our days were mainly filled with training, we had Wednesday afternoons off. In the late summer heat, we were drawn down to the Hoe because we were teenagers and we wanted to try all the things that the normal ones did.

'Don't you think it looks a bit stupid not matching?' said Amelia to no one in particular, the top of the bikini puckered slightly around the cheap gold ring that held it all together and was digging into her flat chest. The bottoms were bright pink, unlike the fake denim of the top, cut tight against the back of her glutes and loose and baggy at the front where the V-shape muscles cut away and the top of her pelvis fell concave between her hips. Our feet were cold and hard on the rocks, and around the old diving board slippery green algae gripped the rust where the poles of its frame met the concrete. It stood to the left-hand side of where we were sitting, with the sun harsh behind it. Everyone was jumping off and the girls had Maybelline water- proof mascara on and fake tan left over from holidays and late nights in the park. Amelia and I got in the water again and it felt like my organs were going to shut down; the sun had warmed my skin too much and the water felt like needles now against my goose-bumped arms. Some of them had grown up on the coast here, but the water was 30°C colder than the Indian Ocean I was used to. We stayed sheltered from the current and the waves in L-shapes on our backs, panting, hyperventilating. The waves rocked us back and forth and the sun made it feel like we could stay in for just a little bit longer. It was hot for late August, it had to be really hot to go down to the Hoe, and when the afternoon started to cool slightly, we pulled our hair up onto our heads and sunned ourselves in our cheap bikinis, and from a spot on the rocks we watched the boys jump off the diving board.

Jenkins smiled at me over Dan's head. They were down near the bottom of the steps and the rest of the boys were standing around them. I guess that's when they had the idea. They were going to swim to the island – Drake's, it was called, after a privateer who used it to defend England from its invaders. It had been a place of pilgrimage, then refuge, then defence and finally imprisonment. The prison stood proudly near the water's edge in a building that had originally been a chapel. Built on a small green crop of land, it looked like a digital fortress from *Age of Empires*, or an accidental discovery in *Swallows and Amazons*: not a real place, small and idyllic, with falling-down stone structures and a wooden jetty just visible from our vantage point. It was just a bit too far away to look real. But you could see the beach, which looked close enough, and the sandbank around the island turned the water around its shores an inviting turquoise. This enticing sand and bright blue water continued all the way across the bay to our feet and stopped just beneath the rocks we were sitting on. Flat water and a tiny breeze and floods of sunshine, maybe it didn't seem so far away after all. Like the length of an average warm-up in training – turn off your brain and swim freestyle for a while, just with no wall and no tumble turns for rest. I said it wasn't a good idea, but not loudly enough. They had already gone.

When the sun was almost level with the horizon, a coastguard boat came into view. We had wrapped our towels round our legs for warmth and the fading light had hidden our worry from each other. The boys were still in their trunks, teeth chattering, laughing to mask their cold as the coastguards helped them off the boat onto shore a little further around the rocks, where the water was deeper.

'What the fuck, guys!' Sara rounded on them as they arrived back where they'd started and we were still sitting – the older girls were standing now. 'That was pretty stupid, don't you think?' – 'We told you we would make it,' Dan replied, 'and we did make it to the beach, but some people struggled with the temperature, didn't they?' He jerked his head over towards two of the boys in my year. One of them, Cameron, was new this year; he was shivering silently. Amelia had started collecting all the boys' things together. Sara started up the long concrete steps in a huff, and I stood looking at Cameron. He was only a little bit taller than me, and the thinness of his face was matched through the rest of his body. We had similar physiques, all sinew and no fat, skin pulled so tightly over our stomachs that there wasn't even any spare to let our belly buttons cave in. Every muscle on his body was visible, and spreading out from the soft space underneath his cupid's bow was a dark blue stain as if he'd been sucking on a board marker; it took me a while to realise that it was his oxygen-less blood, icy and advancing like a disease. 'Let's go!' Dan shouted. Amelia had three of the boys' soggy towels over her shoulder and she was holding her trainers as she went past me quickly barefoot. She didn't wait. I walked over to where Cameron was leaning. 'We have to go.' I looked at him, he nodded but his eyes wouldn't focus. 'Come on.' I pulled him by the top of his arm.

Up on the roadside there was more light. The fear and the water had made our spot on the Hoe seem darker than the summer evening actually was and the sodium glow from the old seaside streetlamps emboldened Dan and one or two of the other boys. I was walking at the back with Cameron, who was breathing very slowly. I thought it was just shock. As we walked on, I could hear Dan boasting up ahead. The pavement on the right-hand side of the road cut into a grey stone bank which held a grassy mound above that led into town. Cameron was trailing his arm along the wall, both pulling himself forward and keeping himself upright.

'Guys, come on, wait!' Some of the sixth-formers were just in front of us. I called out to them, 'I think he has hypothermia;

I'm not joking, we should probably call the boarding house or something, can one of you do it?' Some heads turned and one of the girls looked at Cameron and then back at me. 'Why would I call? You know who's on duty this evening as well!' she snapped back at me. 'Look, he's walking fine. You're going to be fine, right, Cameron?' He mumbled back at her in response. 'See?' she said triumphantly. At first I thought she was joking, but when she turned around, I realised that of course our pact was we would always be fine, so long as no one said anything. 'Can you just get Dan, please, will you just get him then?' They were ignoring me now and so I reached out instead to touch Amelia's arm, 'Please,' I implored. Cameron was shivering audibly now. Whether he had been making any effort to curb it before I didn't know, but his whole body was shaking, and he was moaning slightly. 'Are you okay?' I asked as I half looked behind while trying to keep my other eye trained on Amelia and Dan at the front. I saw her point and Dan looked over his left shoulder back at us.

We'd made very little progress; everyone was walking slowly to mask the fact that Cameron was only putting one foot in front of the other every time he exhaled. I thought about my mum, all the times I'd told her that something had spilled or ripped; and about the teachers I'd apologised to on behalf of the class after everyone had gone out for break, and my sister, who I'd pulled from the bottom of a pool four years ago half-dead, and I got my phone out. I was looking down at the tiny screen when Dan rounded on me. Cameron was slumped against the wall, and I had my hand on his shoulder half propping him up. 'Let's just get back and it'll be fine.' I could hear the worry in Dan's voice. 'I'm calling an ambulance, he's obviously not okay!' I replied. I didn't look up because my lip was trembling. 'Listen, you cunt, if you tell anyone this was my fault, I'm gonna be fucking livid,' Dan snarled at me. 'I'm not gonna say anything,' I replied through a clenched jaw and then I looked up at him defiantly to make sure he knew I was done talking. He turned away and I dialled 999.

After the ambulance came, they wrapped Cameron in a silver blanket and got his parents' number and asked a couple of questions, then they took him away. He would be fine now.

We traipsed the rest of the way back to the boarding house in silence. We all knew we were really in trouble and that we weren't allowed to give detail on what had happened; of course, it had been Dan's idea, but no names were given either. I didn't tell my mum. We had all got into the habit of keeping everything a secret from anyone who might have offered a perspective that wasn't punitive: we believed we deserved to be punished, and our parents probably wouldn't have agreed. After the Drake's swim no one was exempt, and the punishment was harder training – I think they liked it when we broke the rules; it meant control could tighten. We had tried to be kids, but we'd coloured too far outside the lines; we'd done it wrong and broken at least two dozen rules in the process. How well you followed the rules determined how committed you were, and we were told that our commitment to the club, the commitment that had been specifically outlined for us, was the most important ingredient to our success. 'Do you want to be here or not?'

Roan would ask, if you forgot to bring a bottle with you to training. If you answered no, which that specific day may have been exactly how you felt, then why were you here at all, why had you trained every day for the last ten years only to forget your bottle? And if you answered yes, you *did* want to be there; well, if that were true, you wouldn't've forgotten your bottle, would you? This happened often enough that eventually you imposed the rules on yourself – that was the idea. Like crated dogs, ultimately the whining ceased and each evening, without coercion, we'd slink back to our crates and lock ourselves in, accepting all the rules we'd signed up to when we came here: athletes must complete a log book, athletes/parents must not plan any family holidays that fall during the season, athletes who do not attend morning sessions (when expected) are not to attend the afternoon session on the same day. This was the shape of the rules, and the list was endless. But they seemed tame compared to the one that Roan, I felt, imposed on us wordlessly every day: don't think that you are anything unless I make you into something.

X

Sometimes we were wrong, but mostly we could always tell it was coming. Often, we only did it once or twice a month and only in the first part of the season, three or four times in total. But after the Drake's swim, we did it three weekends in a row: 60 × 100 metres. I had never done the set before I got to Plymouth that year. It felt barbaric: intellectually challenging and physically taxing in a way that almost nothing else came close to, and it was impossible to finish. There was always a rumour that someone had seen someone else finish the set a couple of years before. I never believed that anyone could complete the whole thing, until I watched Jenkins do it that year. The 60 × 100 metres set is almost as hard to coordinate as it is to swim; the coach needs four stopwatches running at the same time and an assistant coach to note down how many have been completed. Every 100 metres the turnaround time gets one second faster; the first 100 metres is off two minutes, which means the sixtieth lap, if you make it that far, has to be swum under one minute to complete the whole thing. A drop-out set, that's what Roan called it: you swim until you don't make the turnaround and the goal is to hold on for as long as you can. A good number for the girls was about 48, and for the oldest boys it was around 55. The hardest thing about 60 × 100 metres is speeding up at the right time: too early and you use up too much energy, too late and you can't get yourself going enough when the turnaround times get faster. A nervous, jittery energy hangs over the pool at the beginning of this set; no one wants to drop out early, in full view of the rest of the squad, carrying the embarrassment through the rest of the weekend with everyone being slightly distant from you, not wanting to be infected by your poor performance. There's inter-competition too, beating the person who hung on just one more lap than you could last time and vice versa, or making sure you beat the person who's gunning for you. You're also expected to beat whatever number you managed the last time the set was swum. Like all sets designed to test you on multiple fronts, there are a hundred different tactics. Normally, I would do the first 10 with a kickboard, nice and easy with my goggles on my head chatting to Cameron in the next lane, then 11 to 30 change to backstroke, gulping down as much air as possible trying to feel for the exact moment my heart rate jumped up above resting, this usually came by number 28, and then I'd change to freestyle and prepare for the sharp jolt down in the amount of rest I had at the end of each 100 metres. It started to get hard at 40, the turnaround time now one minute twenty seconds. It was time to get going.

'Turn on the legs!' Julia is screaming from the top of the pool. Number 42. Breathe, breathe, breathe, go. Holding onto the wall with my right hand, I pull myself up by my bicep and fingers, then push hard with my feet and flick one hand over my head to meet the other. Choppy waves from the boys up ahead pushed me off-centre as my head broke the surface. I was breathing towards the side of the pool Julia was standing on and she put both her hands out, palms up, and alternated moving them up and down. She meant kick. Harder. I obeyed. Five more times I ploughed my arms overhead and breathed again, my head towards her. Julia was holding her stopwatch straight up in the air with one hand and with the other she made a sweeping motion as if she were brushing everything off a desk onto the floor. That meant, hurry the fuck up because you're not going to make it. Number 43: I wasn't dropping out at 43, even Sinead hadn't dropped out yet. Time to move. I hit the wall hard. With 50 metres to go, I pushed eight fly kicks underwater and came up in a different gear. It was time for an eight-beat kick, my legs alternating eight times to every one arm stroke; like a motorboat I churned up white water around my ankles. Jenkins had pushed off and was underwater next to me, already going in the opposite direction starting the next lap. The pool was so hot that the chlorine was starting to change state. A thick mist like stratus clouds hung for a metre above the surface of the water and the gaseous chlorine caught in my throat and stung my eyes through my goggles. 'Ready, uhhp.' Julia sent off the second group, five seconds after the first and just as I touched the wall. She was standing over my lane. I had time for four breaths, that was it. I took them as she hissed at me, 'I expect at least another ten, at least.'

The 4½ kilometres I had put behind me in less than an hour and a half were starting to show up in my shoulders; I couldn't speed my arms up, and my frantic feet were driving my head further and further down as if they would propel me to the bottom. I windmilled in desperation, throwing my hands over my head and at the pool in front of me. There was nothing but the ten-second gap now between me and Jenkins, only seven of us left in the whole pool; the drop-outs had thrown the doors open and the water cooled, sucking the chlorine clouds back into it. I was bargaining with myself: just make two more then you can stop. I never did manage to keep going until I missed the time. Pride, control, I didn't know. But I did know that I couldn't make it to 60, and I wouldn't, that was a fact. If I couldn't do it, I would rather it were me than the clock that decided when it ended. 52. I had less than two seconds on the wall. 'Go, go, go!' Julia waved me on. Every 100 metres I went on like this and the bargaining continued.

I was the only girl left in the pool, so I'd won that game at least. Did I have enough in me to beat Cameron? We were the only two Year Tens left, and we were in the second session that morning, already at an advantage because we knew how many everyone in the early session had done. As we pushed on through number 53, I realised Cameron would push on to beat Jack, who'd managed 53 in the session before us. 'Seven, six, five, four, three . . .' Everyone on poolside was counting down, they did that when it got tight and I was about to miss the turnaround. Decision time. One more. I touched the wall. 'Go!' shouted Julia immediately.

Even if I were going to stop after this one, in order for it to count I had to swim under one minute and six seconds. Number 54. I closed my eyes as my head went under and I flipped my feet towards the wall at the end of the first length. Tumble turn. I went to push off and the wall wasn't there, I'd missed it; the exhaustion had stolen my spatial awareness. That push-off was crucial. I was a body length behind Cameron now, with just under three lengths to go. 'How do you win, how do you win, how do you win?' I harassed myself. 'Come on.' I snap my head up and find another gear, a gear only I have. 'You do what they can't,' I answer. I hammer down the pool and by the next turn I'm at Cameron's shoulder. He didn't have another one in him and we both knew this was the end when he moved in towards the lane rope and breathed towards me. That meant, come on, I will go with you, I will take you there. I matched his rhythm; breathing every two strokes we used each other's inertia, I felt like he was pulling me along the red plastic discs, one at a time, as we hacked up the last length of the pool. Everyone was cheering us. Jenkins was long gone for 55. 'Three, two, one—' We touched the wall and both immediately looked over to Julia: two thumbs up. I turned to Cameron, he smiled, and I did too. Then I got out of the pool and walked through the double glass doors and threw up on the path outside.

*

By the time I was fourteen, I was in the top fifty female breaststrokers in the world, not just for my age; a year later I would be in the top five. For Christmas I was back down in South Africa for the All-Africa Games. A bloated South African team battled it out against Tunisia for the top position in the medal table. Apart from the white Africans, like the girl who swam for Zimbabwe, no other nation won swimming medals and the finals were seldom close. I didn't want to be there as much as I didn't want to be at the boarding house back in Plymouth, but like all things now, it wasn't a choice. My mum came down to meet me in South Africa and did my economics project while I slept in the hours between heats and finals. I had barely engaged with school that last term; it was the first year of my GCSEs and I was reading *Grazia* magazine in class, hidden inside my grey plastic Physics folder. 'What's going on, Achieng?' my mum asked me as we got ready to leave for the pool again. 'Nothing, I just need my inhaler,' I replied as I pulled everything out of my bag again and held back burning tears of frustration. Swimming had given me asthma, slowly, over the course of the last four years; my lungs were huge but overused and already getting tired. The altitude here didn't help. I had two golds already but tonight I had to swim the relay, the anchor leg. 'These girls have never won any international medals; this could be incredible for them and for Kenya,' my mum was nattering like she always did when I got nervous and silent, but her words burrowed into me intensely today, and I resented her and my place in the world and everyone else in it too. We were ranked fourth into the final and it was up to me to get us onto the podium.

I didn't understand what I had done when I won in Johannesburg that week with a sullen face and uninspiring attitude. Withdrawn and institutionalised, I hated my routine and hated being out of it even more. I was even starting to hate being back in Africa, being reminded that I was different from everyone back in Plymouth – like I didn't feel it enough every day. When I won the 50- and 100-metre breaststroke events at the All-Africa Games that year, I became the first Kenyan woman to win medals at any major international swimming meet, ever. And our bronze in the Women's 4 × 100-metre freestyle relay put us in the history books again. But I had misunderstood everything that was wrong with my sport in Africa: I thought (through my own internalised racism) that African swimming was unserious, rather than underfunded, and that this competition was a joke, a distraction from the real thing. I felt like it was pulling me under. I had been the best here for so long that it had stopped mattering to me; they were all holding me back, like my sisters who'd caged me in my brown skin, my Kenyan nationality kept me shackled to a boat I felt I was single-handedly rowing.

Just before New Year, my mum had found an article by the Kenyan *Standard*; they wrote that after that Games I was set to be one of Africa's greatest female swimmers of all time. Penny Heyns' African record was in sight, and the article mentioned Zimbabwean Olympic medallist Kirsty Coventry too. It didn't mention that the other two greatest African female swimmers were white. I was on the precipice of breaking Penny's record in the 50-metre breaststroke, which had stood since 1996. She was a legend, a double Olympic champion, the first to win both the 100-metre and the 200-metre event.

I would go on to break the record at the end of that same season, five months after my fourteenth birthday, in August 2009. And it was only then that I indulged in my first moment of uncritical hope, a dream that was becoming real as I swam it into existence. I didn't want to be one of the greatest African swimmers of all time, this thought seeped out of me in child-like arrogance: no, I wanted to be the greatest ever.

XI

I always had fried bread as well as hash browns, because I was vegetarian. The canteen had a chequerboard MDF ceiling, alternating between squares of bright white light and mottled grey panels. A never-ending counter with large pill-shaped silver trays sat under the electric orange glow of the warming lights above them. The front of the counter was black vinyl with bright yellow stickers at regular intervals; in black outlined triangles, four thin lines of steam rose from a thick base that had an arrow pointing down at it: caution, hot surface. The normal boarders' breakfast slot was early, but the dinner ladies, whom we knew by name, made a separate breakfast for us after we'd finished training and we had the whole canteen to ourselves. Two eggs, mushrooms, beans – never the half-boiled whole tomatoes – two pieces of fried bread if you could swing it and at least one hash brown, and sometimes pancakes; those were good mornings. I loved feeling full. The boys always got there first, apart from Cameron and one other boy in our year, who were both from up north and put gel in their hair and something other than Lynx on their bodies.

We walked over from the pool without our blazers on, warm in the May morning, past the big cream building with the sixth-form centre and the headmaster's office in it and the red-brick to its side, where the nurse had two single beds that we'd sometimes sleep in during the day, if we could convince her that we weren't well enough to be in class. At the top of that building, Roan had a small office in the eaves with a slopping roof and an old computer in the corner. The pleated folds in Sara's long blue skirt were softly blowing open and closed like window blinds. I watched her and Kayli as they walked along the path in front of me, my tartan skirt shorter because our uniforms were different; I was still in lower school. 'Guys, wait.' I turned to see Abi, who was with Kat and had called out from behind me to the girls up ahead.

Dan and Jenkins were seated at the table closest to both the door and the food counter while a short, thin long-distance swimmer with a canine face was talking about a film they'd all watched that weekend. I'd spoken to him quite a lot: he liked school – unlike most of the swimmers – like I did before it had started to create friction between me and the pool. I didn't know why he still swam; he didn't seem built for it with his sloping shoulders, and although he was great in training, he never competed well. But there were a couple like that in our group. It didn't seem like their parents pushed them, and it wasn't clear if Roan and Julia cared whether they were there or not, but they were easily as committed as the rest of us. Despite this, they barely qualified for the Nationals. Their swimming careers weren't going anywhere beyond that annual meet in Sheffield, and they knew it, but each season they carried on. 'Yeah, well, even if the girlfriend hadn't been a shitty double agent, it still wasn't a good film.' Jenkins was laughing as Dan carried on and started acting out a shooting scene. 'Also, like, why did it have to replay from exactly the same point every time?' He wasn't really asking. – 'Because,' the other boy paused, '. . . because it's literally called *Vantage Point*!' He looked at Dan and there was a longer pause, then Dan's self-assured bark, and they all laughed. It seemed so easy for them.

My crispy fried bread leaked a pool of oil around my mush-rooms as I drowned it under baked beans. Abi and Kat were sitting at the table next to the boys and I was sitting with the other younger swimmers one table away again. We mostly sat in year groups at breakfast, but there were only ever eighteen of us at any given morning training. 'Are you going to see him tonight?' Kat to Abi, her large teeth spilling over her tongue as the girls continued to talk about nothing. Dan scraped his chair back and sat with his legs spread wide, tossing an apple in the air. The boys were almost finished. I started inhaling my food so I could slip out before them and with one eye on the girls too, making sure we didn't have to walk out together or that they weren't whispering about something I was doing that wasn't quite right. I was almost finished when Cameron came in and sat down next to me.

Everyone was waiting for someone else to leave first when

Jenkins stood up quickly. He made direct eye contact with me as he pulled on his blazer, dark blue unlike mine; he was in his first year of sixth form. Unmoving, I looked back at him. 'Are you going right now?' Dan asked loudly, looking up at him. Loud enough that the girls stopped talking. Jenkins didn't answer. I bit my lip as Cameron said my name for the third time. 'Sorry, yeah, yeah, what?' I leaned my head towards him but kept my eyes fixed on the boys' table. Cameron was talking to me about something to do with our form tutor and double French later today and a new boy who was starting. Jenkins found my eyes again and cocked his head very subtly towards the door. I got up without saying anything, my heart loud in my ears, and the hum of the warming lights seemed to have been dialled up as well. Behind the counters was a long row of windows and behind that a courtyard; it created a covered corridor just outside the canteen that ended in three stone steps that led down to a main thoroughfare, an artery that took you to anywhere in the school's grounds. It was just about to get busy. School hadn't started yet, but in seven minutes the first people would be walking past.

Silhouetted at the end of the corridor, Jenkins was waiting for me. The rubber soles of my shoes were nearly silent on the smooth stone floor. He didn't turn around until I was only a couple of metres behind him. When he smiled at me, I felt like a different person. But I also knew I wasn't that person – most days I was sure my lack of whiteness stopped me from being her, and so it felt like a horrible mistake, one I was waiting for him to realise he'd made, and I ruined the relationship with this insecurity almost immediately. But that morning, he stepped backwards down two stairs so that his face was level with mine, his broad frame held my forearms without effort as I rested them on his shoulders and laced my hands together behind his head. He put his hands on my hips, inside my blazer on my rayon jumper, his fingers almost touching around my small waist as he pulled me closer. I could hear Dan and the others making whooping noises, and I could feel the girls' eyes on us through the canteen window. I hadn't told anyone after we'd talked outside the bathroom stalls last night near the common room, and I guess he hadn't either. His hands tightened around me and suddenly his hair was against my cheek. Cloves and chlorine and Nivea. He whispered in my ear, his deep voice soft like his damp hair, 'Are you going to have a good day?' I didn't answer. My hands were in his hair now, pulling him closer so that he didn't look at me too closely. I hated that he was perceiving me, the visibility of the moment, it was mortifying, but I never wanted it to end. 'Do you think it will be okay or is it going to be weird for you now?' I said quietly into his neck. His bottom lip was slightly bigger than his top, puffy and deep pink and a little dry. It brushed my jaw as he found my lips in response to my question. It wasn't our first kiss, but it did feel like the first real one, here in full view of everyone. I could feel my hair starting to dry and imagined it puffing slightly, pulling against my hairband, the hyperpigmentation under my arms from constantly shaving, prune-coloured and shameful. I didn't believe he really liked me, and I knew I never would. 'I'll see you at training tonight,' he said as I walked off in the direction of my form room, and I didn't look back as I could hear the girls running and calling after me.

*

'You're not going to be able to go home this year. Maybe for a week over August but it's going to be back-to-back, and I think the Grand Prix is going to be really important for us,' Roan said with his back to me. I was missing the last period before lunch, standing in the doorway of his office as he printed off the entry form for me to sign. He looked too big in every room, and this was no exception. Pale auburn hair so light it was almost blond, and stubble just the same colour. He had no jawline and his eyes were set deep into his large face, all his features occupying only a quarter of this expansive real estate, his eyes sometimes creased with steeliness that for some might pass for cruelty, thin and sloping and pale green under paler eyebrows. If I looked at him for long enough, when everyone else had looked away, I would always find what looked like a smirk that danced around the right corner of his mouth; subtle and fleeting, it was his only tell. In that moment I thought that the depth of his ambition was contained in that small line that ran from the edge of his sharklike nose to the point where his bottom and top lip joined.

'What?' He had turned to look at me and had caught me watching him. 'I don't know, I'm just thinking about Nationals as well, I guess. I'm gonna miss half of it anyway. Do I really have to go?' I looked up at him and tried to smile as he brought the warm, freshly printed paper over to me. – 'Look, I don't really care about age-group Nationals, but Julia wants you there. Whatever, we'll have some fun when you get to Worlds.' He turned back to the large monitor, and I thought about the World Championships later that year, arguably the biggest event after the Olympics and maybe even more competitive. I thought about the perfect bodies of all the swimming celebrities who would be there. Roan was crunched up in his chair, his long back curved over: its mass couldn't be contained by his shoulder blades and was almost spilling into the bottom of his hairline, creating small hills of fat that angulated at the back of his neck. I stretched instinctively on the top of the door frame, my palms pushing forwards, opening my shoulder blades up like wings as my shirt rode up, my protruding ribcage pulling the stretchy cotton apart. 'Tone looks good.' Roan had turned back to me again and was looking at the line running from my belly button down to the tights folded over the top of my skirt. 'Fat-testing tomorrow,' he announced, as he reached out to his mouse and moved it back and forth, 'with the full machine and sticky pads. Tell Sara to cut . . . Actually, don't tell Sara anything, she could do with a sharp shock.' His huge shoulders shrugged briefly as he let out a single laugh.

Between the door to the pool and the old gym was the outside, and the fresh air underscored the smell we largely didn't register anymore. Sweet, like trampled honeysuckle flowers mixed with small balls of cotton wool dipped in bleach, the smell of natural body oil and urine converting into gas by the heat of all our bodies in the pool, with the top note of bathroom cleaner, and it drifted up, to travel with me always, the most enduring smell of my life: chlorine. After training that day, we put on our gym kit – sports bras and very short shorts – and walked past that door to the outside and into the old gym. Our assistant coach loved this day, maybe because she had an undergrad degree in sports science, more likely because she was overweight herself. I was fourteen still and my period wasn't even on the horizon, and I didn't have an inch of fat on me, no boobs either, still, to my dismay. I could see Sinead and Sara leaning behind the wall – they never talked, I couldn't remember the last time I'd seen Sara be friendly with anyone outside her group, but I recognised this as a moment of solidarity. The wall fell away at chest height, it was cut out for spectators, creating a shelf which they leaned forward against, and the skin either side of Sara's armpits folded over itself in four neat pleats, like her school skirt. I played netball in here; I loved to move, every sport appealed to me still, and since I was half naked all the time and my body looked like it did, I didn't think about what I looked like when I was exercising. Sinead kept a baggy T-shirt on until it was her turn, its sleeves ending where the strawberry-dappled redness coated the underside of her arms. She walked with her feet almost turned in. I didn't like watching the other girls being weighed. The staff did it in front of everyone, then stuck small electro-pads to our arms, stomach and legs; they were crocodile-clipped to wires that plugged into a small machine with a calculator screen. Sinead's was much higher than mine, and Sara's was much higher still. They always cried, Sinead's face contorted and red, just like in our sessions. I didn't understand why they didn't just keep up the running like Roan and our assistant coach would force them to do. It only ever lasted a week and then I would see them on the way back from Somerfield with a plastic bag of hidden treats and a full jar of chocolate spread; an almost-empty jar lurked in the boarding-house kitchen, put there as a test. We were hungry all the time. I didn't understand that their hormones made this a rigged battle and almost impossible. I had always been thin, and I had always eaten a lot. Roan's words stuck in my head, and I watched Sara cry with curiosity.

Abi, Kat and I were last to get changed after the testing. Sara gave them a look that I couldn't interpret as she walked out. I pulled my Superdry trackies straight over my shorts. 'Are you not gonna get changed properly?' Abi asked me across the stalls. – 'Erm, I don't . . .' I shrugged and let my sentence fall away. – 'I bet you don't even have hair down there,' Kat followed up from nowhere. I stood in my sports bra and shorts, unsure if I'd heard her properly as my brain refused to translate what she'd just said into something I could comprehend. I knew they didn't really like me, but nothing like this much. 'Of course I have hair down there,' I said shakily. Abi laughed. – 'Well, if you do, you'll show us, won't you?' Kat stood up and came towards me. 'No,' I retorted, 'of course I'm not going to show you.' I took the tiniest step back and hoped Kat hadn't noticed. – 'Well, that's probably because you don't. I bet you don't even need to shave,' Kat replied. I stared at her blankly and held her gaze, then took my trackies off again and let a long, pregnant silence follow as they stood looking at my body, the small, round, sticky circles still visible on my stomach from the pads, and I stood looking back at them in my tiny Lycra shorts and red T-back sports bra. I thought about getting completely undressed so they actually *could* see; but as quickly as I'd had the thought, I spun round, then bent to pick up my trainers. 'Take my bag to the bus, I'm going to run back.' I didn't look at either of them as I said it, my face burning and inside an embarrassment so total it was overflowing, running out of my nose and ears down onto my neck, dripping down my jaw. As I walked out of the sports centre, I saw Jenkins on the bus. He had an empty seat beside him and he might have been about to wave to me through the window, but I didn't wait to see. I turned and walked quickly to the main entrance of the school, breaking into a run just before the gate. My jaw clenched and arms pumping, the sun dappled through the emerging leaves and the town becoming greyer and greyer the faster I ran past it, until I got to the long length of the wall that surrounded Graige Drive.

'Please, Mum.' I was still out of breath, the phone sweaty against my cheek, 'Please, I don't want to do this, I hate it here, please, I just want to come home!' My voice was vibrating. 'Oh, my love, but you're doing so well, at school, your times this season.' She was probably sitting in the living room. I closed my eyes to picture it better. 'Please, Mum,' I whispered. – 'What's happened, Achi, tell me?' she implored. – 'I just – I just hate it.' There was nothing else to say, there was nothing else there when I reached inside myself.

XII

I watched the finals with the British Swimming team, next to Roan in my fake Wayfarer Ray-Bans, standing out in the sea of blue, red and white, me in a muddy green T-shirt with a small Kenyan flag embroidered over my right breast and my brown skin almost deep orange in the Italian sun. The 13th World Swimming Championships were held in Rome that summer, from the end of July through early August, on the site of an old Olympic stadium. They had built the competition pool just for the Championships, on a raised platform with a temporary 50-metre box sunk into the middle and rickety stands all around, like the Coliseum in the distance. The rest of the facilities were original, and the whole swim-down pool was carved out of marble, the sides seamlessly becoming grey marble steps that trickled between huge columns of veiny blue-grey stone that led out to the top of the stadium. It was one of the most beautiful things I had ever seen, a feat of pure aesthetic indulgence, and the first time I walked through the entranceway I knew I would never forget the feeling of being in that endless room of marble with a swimming pool cut into the floor. Ryan Lochte got into my marble lane on the first day of the competition and asked me which direction we were swimming round in – at least, that's what I imagined he said to me when I retold the story to the Newcastle girls a week later back in the UK. On the 1st of August I swam the heats of the 50-metre breaststroke. It had been one of the longest seasons of my life and my legs and back were shredded with tiny lacerations all through my over-developed muscles. I came twentieth, missing the semi-final by four places in a time of 31.63: a personal best. At some point in the last three years, almost without my realising, I had become a legitimate athlete on the world swimming circuit. But because I was still competing for Kenya and I'd been at championships like these since I was twelve, disregarded as a wild-card African swimmer, just there for representation, it was completely overlooked by almost everyone, and by me most of all. I wasn't placing and I wanted everything the top girls had; they were still swimming almost a second faster than me.

The final line-up could have been guessed: two Australians, three Canadians, two from the USA and a seventeen-year-old Russian girl who went on to take gold. Two years later, she was banned for doping and then again before the next Olympics. The vicious scandal followed her all the way to the podium in a Cold War stand-off with the American who eventually out-touched her on the wall to take a clean gold. In Rome it was the era of the racing suit. Full-body, shoulder-to-ankle sealskins so tight you could barely breathe when someone in the call room zipped you in just minutes before your race, a rubberised silicone that had to be dragged together to close at the top, catching the soft, tiny hairs on your back as the zip chased the black lining upwards and ripped them in clumps from your skin. The full-body tech suits, as they were called in retrospect, saw world record after world record fall; most often to those with the most power, especially the heavier girls whose mass they compressed and buoyed, leaving only their sheer strength undisturbed as they ripped themselves down the pool, swimming on top of the water as the suits' tiny air pockets filled. Mine was bright pink, a Jaked, over a thousand pounds of synthetic advantage. My skin puckered at its edge at the bottom of my thigh. Stars and stripes covered the Americans' suits and maple leaves their northern cousins. The Australians had bright green and gold costumes, sponsored by the best brands of the moment. By the time I was fifteen, my mum could have bought two brand-new Skodas with what she'd spent on my racing suits; and she paid my flights for every competition I attended for Kenya: Senegal, South Africa, Mexico, Manchester, now Rome, as well as my accommodation, and all the rest of my kit, including our team uniform. Mistakenly, I thought the whole team paid their own way, but we weren't all the same.

I looked down at my sandal and felt the liquid that had just been poured onto my foot turn immediately sticky between my toes in the heat of the late summer evening. The music was

loud, and lights flashed against a mirrored floor. On a roof
terrace somewhere in Campo di Fiori, in the very centre of
Rome, Omega was hosting the closing party, and all the best
athletes in the swimming world were spilling drinks on the
reflective dancefloor between small cabaret tables covered in
Omega monogrammed tablecloths. Roan was in the corner,
head down in conversation with the former Director of USA
Swimming, who had just been appointed the National Head
Coach of the British team. He was suspiciously tanned, bald,
and handsome once, with taut skin stretched across a strong
nose, and his stronger Alabama accent carried across the room.
I had neither a team nor the drinking age on my side as my
enduring self-consciousness led my hand up to the back of my
head, trying to stroke the humidity out of my growing hair.
The Kenyan team was just me and the two older guys, brothers,
both white Kenyans born into a family that had long outgrown
their expat roots. They spoke Swahili fluently and their dad
was our team manager. I heard the American's voice again:
'She's only fifteen, that's pretty good, is she locked in . . .' He
trailed off as the music surged. One of the brothers came up
to me and pushed his hip into mine, 'Achi, come on, are you
dancing?' He put both his arms out and bopped his head
ironically. He was attractive in a way that felt permanently out
of reach, like all the men who won and kept winning their
whole lives; tall, over 6 foot 5, with surfer-blond hair and a
smile that crinkled the skin around his eyes and teeth you
couldn't buy. My whole world now was made up of men who
looked like this, with perfect bodies and big hands who looked

at me like I was a foreign object. He danced away and the floor reflected a thousand white tanned legs around me moving slowly with the music; in the reflection I also saw something else, Roan's finger pointing towards the edge of the roof, the mirrored floor confused its direction, and I looked up to find him so I could follow it. He was still talking to the American, but he was pointing at me.

Exactly four days before my swim in Rome I'd been in Sheffield at the British ASA Youth Championships, and for the first time, I had swum a perfect race. Five seconds faster than anyone else in my semi-final. They might as well not have been there; I didn't need them. It was just me, the wall, the crowd, my legs, my soft mind, and years of grit, a thousand lengths, and a hundred early dawns, the clink of the metal weights bar, and so many numbers called out to me from a stopwatch over and over; they all added up to this. 1.08.60. Despite it being an age-group competition, I was now ranked first in the UK. I'd climbed shaky and beaming out of the pool, down the far side and then back behind the block to collect my clothes from the small box next to a chair behind my lane. I looked to the end of the pool, and standing parallel to me with her arms outstretched, ushering me to her, was my coach, Julia. Ponds Forge pool is a basement. Tired and dating fast, coated in blue plastic. But in that moment, it felt like the centre of the world, and everyone was there just for me. We started to walk towards the other end of the pool, me gripping onto Julia's arm; she was propping me upright and I was heaving. Everyone was on their feet, people put their arms out as we walked past, leant down from the stands, calling my name, shouting 'well done' and 'incredible swim!' I saw all the faces I'd got to know over the past two years and felt the tables turn as I walked past. Jealousy, admiration, longing; and I didn't care. I had a new-found distance from them all, because now I really was the best. My racing costume was unspeakably tight, and as I got back to the area where our club was sitting I started to pull at the straps and manoeuvre my shoulders up and down to twist my arms out of it, tucking them into the body and folding it over until it looked like a strapless top. Our assistant coach came over to take my lactic acid levels. A sharp needle to the softest part of my ear lobe, a tiny drop of blood onto the tongue of the small machine, and a sarcastic remark about something. Too much celebrating, not enough, before anyone else had finished the race, or after, something about the way I had won, which everyone always seemed to care about and I not at all. The win and the medal seemed as trivial to me as it ever could have and with the adrenaline still hot in my hands, I slipped into the diving pit to swim down.

Another morning began at the Holiday Inn. An unspectac-ular breakfast followed by a slow walk to the pool. It was cold for July, and I fumbled with my hoodie, faded navy and a bit too small, with our club's emblem in yellow on the right-hand breast. My hair was always wet, dyed jet-black and unnatural despite my brown skin. I pulled up the hood. After five or six days like this it always started to feel like we lived here, at this strange old hotel set on a small hill of concrete surrounded by car parks. It was almost Gothic. A carpeted staircase at least

3 metres wide ran up to the rooms from the reception, its grandness completely out of place; like a film set. We stayed here every year. Sheffield always meant the Holiday Inn. We weren't allowed in each other's rooms, the boys and girls, no mixing. But sometimes we propped our doors open, if we were all on the same corridor, and the boys would wear their speedos and shave down in the bath. The older girls would help them, Sara and Kayli, getting rid of every inch of hair on their bodies, wearing the club trackies and waterproof mascara, on their knees in the hotel bathrooms shaving the backs of the boys' legs.

Ritual was everything at Nationals. I woke up on the final day of racing and knew everyone would be going out that night. I had the same Nutri-Grain bar after breakfast as I always had on race days, and watched one of the boys chew each mouthful of food forty times before swallowing. These strange rituals governed our lives. Some felt exciting and grand at competitions. Most were about need, some about desire, and all were about service. Service to my body, the only asset I had, the only thing that really mattered about me. None of these rituals were very conscious. Trying to fight off age and prevent my period from starting, I wanted to lift more, swim faster, jump higher, recover quicker. Swimmers aren't particularly superstitious, in general; it doesn't help, if you oversleep, miss your warm-up slot or snap the strap of your goggles just before the first whistle – either you race, or you don't. I guess some are superstitious about these things, a little; but not me. I was a performer. I learned very early on that winning was believing.

That's how you win once. But to keep on winning, that was different. To keep on winning, you had to make everyone else believe. To create a myth and perpetuate it yourself. This meant I couldn't buy into superstitious rituals, but it also helped that other people did. If my swimming hat ripped just before my race and everyone saw me calmly leave the call room and get another, the myth grew. That nothing could faze me, that I was unbeatable. Throwing up in the tiled bathrooms just before my call time and stepping up to win once more. There was more power in my myth if I let other people write parts of it too. That I was built differently, that my reaction time after the starting buzzer sounded was 0.23 seconds faster than anyone else's, my Black genes twitching on the block; no one could beat me into the water, people believed this, that I was different. Sometimes I liked that.

The rest of that week had started in a blur of snaking slowly up the tram-lined roads of Sheffield's city centre and buying yum yums on the way to lunch. Then I was to fly to Rome, compete for four days and then straight back for one more competition, the Grand Prix. These were strange and lonely days, not just in the tension between the monotony and intensity of my life in and out of the pool, on and off buses, up and down in planes, but in my knowledge of all these places, even the ones I hadn't been to before, because our routine was always the same. Swimming pool, hotel, airport, swimming pool, hotel, airport: the enduring familiarity of it all. By the end of that week between Sheffield and Rome and with the rest of the season behind me, I would have competed in the 50- and

100-metres breaststroke almost sixty times that year. Every swim was different, painful in new and useful ways, telling me: lift your head faster, do fewer strokes down the first length, kick lighter, squeeze harder, swim. Swim again and again until you can breathe without inhaling, until you can dive without moving, until all that you are is refined into a process that no longer interrogates itself. At the end of all that was the perfect unthinking race, and you, the perfect athlete.

Julia would have had me stay at Youth Nationals until I slowly aged out. I was the big fish in a small 50-metre pool: a technical swimmer, too short to rely on power alone. My strength was in my fast reaction time, quick and springy off the block with a great muscle-to-weight ratio that allowed me to propel myself ahead of others from the very first moments. My jump height was high as well; I needed focus to execute this strong dive, then I needed to get up, not spin my wheels. I was a natural sprinter: the second length didn't come easily to me, so I had to think hard about how I spent my energy down the first. If it had been up to Julia, we would have focused on the long-term until I was at least eighteen: she banished thoughts of 2012 from my mind. 'You're still young,' she'd tell me, 'even for a swimmer. Let's focus on getting those times to keep coming down – physio, technique, drills, you need to keep enjoying in order to swim well.' Roan didn't care about any of that, he wanted to deliver British Swimming the missing piece of the puzzle, the thing that had evaded our national team for years now. A breaststroker, a jewel in the crown of the perfect 4 × 100-metre relay team. The Australians had Jones, the Americans had Soni, the Russians had the seventeen-year-old, and in my generation of British swimmers – they were all at least four years older than me – we had world-class backstroke, freestyle and fly swimmers, but no one on the British team who could compete on a world stage over 100 metres breast-stroke, and with these three girls, dangerously close to ageing out of the sport, Roan knew he had to move fast. The 2012 Olympics were just around the corner, only three seasons away now.

Roan and my mum had been emailing back and forth for months. My swim at Sheffield and my performance in Rome a couple of days later only made him turn the screws faster and harder. Roan would deliver a breaststroker, and he wanted it to be me. He pushed sponsorship, PR companies, throwing the idea of all these contracts at my mum again and again, until eventually she called me one day when I was on the way to the airport. 'Roan wants you to start swimming for Great Britain,' she started. 'I know it's a big thing, love,' she carried on, but I'd stopped listening. Maybe I was useful to Roan beyond my international student fees. Maybe I was going to make his career, not just his swimming club, and propel him off the sidelines and into the action, with all the big old men who went to international conferences and got invited to fancy events in the evening and turned up on poolside to the sound of people whispering their names. 'Achi, are you listening?' my mum asked insistently – she'd believed in Roan at the beginning, and what he might do for me in the sport; she'd sent me to his club because she'd believed she was doing the right thing for me and maybe she still did. 'I said I've spoken to your old coach back in Cape Town. British Swimming are very serious about this. You can't say anything to anyone yet, but I asked him, you know he was always good with thinking about things like this.' I thought about my old coach and imagined him saying the things my mum was recounting to me. 'You won't know how good you can be unless you do this.' I smiled to myself, the image of me in the red, white and blue: the power of that kit, my hand over my left breast mouthing 'God Save the Queen', and they would all see me, when they looked at me, as one of them, they would have to see me then. I thought also of my old coach again, this short Cape Coloured man telling me I had to go and compete in a white space to know if I was really going to make it. He was still coaching in that pool in South Africa with a broken pump and I could see his brown lips cracking as he spoke. 'You have to compete for a place on a team with the best in the world to know if you can set it on fire.'

PART 2

Subside

Taper

XIII

'Then I stood out on a prairie
And as far as I could see
Wasn't nobody on that prairie
That looked like me—'
Langston Hughes

My parents had come over to watch me compete. They arrived on poolside two days before the competition started, but we were already there, warming up. It was a selective international meet, which usually didn't mean anything, except that one or two countries had decided to use it as a qualifier for a bigger international competition, and so it became a head-to-head battle, a 'duel in the pool'. Apart from the World Short Course Championships in Manchester (which I had attended, when I was still too young to pose a threat to anyone), I hadn't been to any real short course meets; competing in a 25-metre pool was much faster than swimming long course in a 50-metre pool. Faster because the walls came more frequently, which allowed for a period of inactivity, followed by a push-off that gave you an advantage every time it came. I hadn't seen my mum for almost six months. We were coming to the end of another training session, trying to stretch out our taper that year because we were still competing despite not having pushed a hard session for almost four weeks. Four weeks of taper. My body was light and twitchy; springy, muscle ebbing away slightly, less bulky than I had been during the long season. I was lighter, from a decreased training volume and also a decrease in food. Taper was mostly for sprinters, and for me it was perfect. 'Well,' Roan had said, 'we've done okay, but the 100 breast is going to be a bit of a risk.' He meant that I probably wasn't fit enough anymore, after a long month of racing and a very significant training-load decrease, to hold on down the last half of the race when the lactic acid would threaten to devour me whole. He was right. I felt weak. Not enough food, not enough mileage in the pool, not enough sleep, and too much rest.

I smiled over at my sisters and my mum as I climbed out down at the far end and walked round the pool towards them. My youngest sister was only three, I had been away most of her life, and she looked at me as if I were a stranger as I approached. I barely knew her either. 'How long are you staying?' I asked my mum, wet and waiting for Roan to call me back round again. I had meant this afternoon at the pool; she looked at me as if she was trying to work out how to step on my hand without it hurting. 'We're going down to the South of France ' she started to say slowly 'You're going down to the South of France?' I heard my voice go up at the end as I repeated her. '—tomorrow,' she finished. – 'Okay, so, you didn't come to Rome, you weren't at Nationals, and now you're here and I'm racing in two days and you're going down to the South of France. Is that right?' I demanded. – 'The girls need a holiday too; they can't just sit on poolside all summer.' Mum lowered her voice and clearly hoped I would join her. – 'When,' I spat, 'have they ever sat on poolside for a summer?' My middle sister's big dark brown eyes, just like mine, were looking from our mum to me. I turned and walked quickly away towards the top of the pool, the agony of their abandonment a new weight on my tired, atrophying body.

I bent down on the block to the sound of commotion behind me – one of the older boys who wasn't at our school but trained with our club was saying my name urgently. At the same time, Roan: 'Take your marks – uhhp!' Confused, I stood up instead of diving on his command and turned round. 'Your tampon string is hanging out,' Lucy leaned forward and told me quietly. My childhood was also gone. Secretly, I was glad it had happened, and that they'd all seen it. Everyone laughed it off, kindly, and for a fleeting moment I felt safe here with these people who had been my constant companions for the last two years – that they knew every inch of my body and had seen every intimacy it hid. There was no embarrassment anymore; there couldn't be. I'd been brutally stripped of privacy and autonomy so completely that the only things I still kept for myself were my virginity and my loneliness. And I was desperate to shed them both. This meet was a wild card for me, the youngest of my team there by almost two years. I had always swum with people older than me because after a short while, in every place I went, I was better than the swimmers my age. But that had mattered much less when I was younger – the age gap had seemed an uncrossable chasm, and I didn't want to grow up then. Now it was only just out of reach. I was fifteen, the older boys were nineteen or twenty and Kayli, my roommate, was now eighteen and about to leave for university. The Grand Prix that year was in Leeds and the Canadian National team was attending, as well as the current British team. On the first night, three world records almost fell. Back at the hotel, Kayli was telling me about a modelling campaign she might be doing soon; we were easy in each other's company when the other older girls weren't around. She talked on as I lay on the cheap hotel bed seething, so righteous in feeling my family's betrayal. I couldn't believe they weren't going to stay to watch me race.

Swimming was a witness to all the things that I was losing and all the things I was becoming in the spaces that loss created. I was starting to feel, without being able to name it, the slow fall-away of all the choices I could have made, and they were falling away because of my choice to swim. So much so that being here had stopped feeling like a choice, because I didn't have any others. Before, my life had been limitless. I was so young, so able and so scared, but the possibility of what I could do, and be, was expansive. Normally, we start to let go of this when we take our first job, move country for a relationship, or get pregnant. Well, this was my first job, my first relationship and my only child. Swimming had taken most of my youth and some of my sisters' too. And as it placed more and more limits on my future, I could feel it constricting around me, tightening its grip on my body; it owned all of my time already, but it owned my future now as well. I looked around me, at the senior swimmers, who all went to one of the small handful of universities in the UK that were attached to high-performance swimming centres; a lot of them didn't make it through university, or it took them years. Some didn't even make it all the way through school. Up ahead I could see some version of my future. I was wedded to it, obsessed by it, unable to stop counting the three years until the summer Olympics and then my scholarship to a college in the US – a result of studying hard – taking me through the four years until Rio 2016 after that. What I did between those years was fading out of view: swimming was the only thing that mattered to those around me. I didn't think about the fact that time would pass and that I might feel differently in three years; I only hoped that my body was still the same, that it could still do the same things, and even better. Swimming was drowning me in hope: I felt waterboarded with optimism and anticipation. But most sacrifices don't account for chance, and certainly not this one. What if your touchpad was just a little bit out of place, half a millimetre further away from the wall than the one in the lane next to you? And what if you'd trained all your youth away and your parents had sacrificed everything and so had you, and you had made it and you were ranked first and you were going to win, but then you didn't? 'Not you,' hope told me, 'that would never happen to you – you're a winner.' A faith stronger than any religion, I had it then, and Roan and my mum and my old coaches and all my gold medals – they made me believe. They encouraged me to let go of any other versions of my life. Not because this would be worth it – there was nothing coming after it and in a way they all knew that. But they didn't care, because we all wanted it so much.

*

When swimming 50 metres breaststroke short course, a world-class race is always going to be over in around thirty seconds. This means if you make a single mistake, even the smallest error, you'll drop 0.5 of a second, and this can be the difference between a good time and a bad time. Mistakes range from a slow reaction time off the blocks (0.6 is fast, 0.8 is slow) to a bad dive (too flat, too high) to a lack of stroke adjustment (you want to hit the first wall at full extension, arms outstretched, legs snapped tight shut straight behind you. If you miscount your strokes, you're too short or too long on the wall). It could be a bad turn (you don't get tight enough, don't get round fast enough, fling your arm too high over the water as you prepare to push off, slip your big toe off the wall as your feet push against it). Over 50 metres breaststroke short course there is one start, one dive, two underwater pull-outs, one turn and one finish. The possibility for mistakes isn't endless, but it's plentiful enough. At more traditional competitions, to mirror the Olympics, it was just the eight fastest into the final, but this was the Grand Prix, a short course invitational shoved at the end of the season, and they were swimming ten-person finals, which was lucky, because my heats swim that morning had been distinctly average. The Canadian girls were faster, older and far more experienced. And I felt sorry for myself, distracted by the fact that my mum's attention was with my sisters by another swimming pool somewhere sunnier and free of rules. I called her in the hours after the heats, sitting alone in my hotel room. The finals were that evening, and I needed someone to tell me that everything was going to be okay. Something was shifting. With an ever-increasing number of stakeholders in my success and eyes I didn't even know watching me intently, I wanted her there to protect me from the doubt that was starting to nibble at the edges of my mind.

'I don't know if I can do this,' I said down the phone as my nerves surged to a swell, but my terror abated as she told me, 'You're going to go out there and do what you do. Julia thinks you can go under 31.00, and I know you can.' She paused. 'Just think about the process.' That's what they'd all say: just focus on the process, let the process lead out, it's about the process, not the outcome. But I loved to win, it made me feel safe. And the process would take me there, but more and more the two things were becoming entangled. The outcome wasn't a happy accident, left to chance or luck: I was expected to win now, even when there was only an outside chance that I could. The Canadian girl who was ranked first into the final was also the world record holder in the 200-metre breaststroke and not far off in the 100 metres. I was ranked fourth and therefore in lane two, closer to the edge of the pool, fighting the choppy water coming out from the middle swimmers: more resistance, which of course meant a harder swim. Did they really think I could win from lane two? But something had taken over, a sneaking suspicion that I was built to win anywhere, and also that I could. The doubt that plagued me was about how powerful this mythology had become, so powerful it had trapped me within it, they had put me inside. It was so important now to my success, to the hope that shrouded how slim a chance this had of ending in the way we all wanted it to, and how easy it would be to shatter the illusion. Only I could keep it intact, feed it by winning again, or harm the armour I had built around myself by failing to produce another impossible swim.

Older swimmers are traditionally better at short course and most of the time they make better sprinters too. Experience builds consistency and makes your swims tighter: fewer mistakes, less time variation, better overall execution. When an experienced sprinter steps up to the blocks, they can often know, almost to the millisecond, how the race will go. I had swum a 31.29 in the morning's heats. I had barely competed in short course at a high level, and I had no idea how much faster I was capable of going, if at all. The Canadian in the middle lane was eleven years older than me, sweet and gracious in the call-room. She saw my nerves. I saw her discount me, so I didn't hide them. Subconsciously, I was always fighting for myself, my body tingling with the atoms of my ancestors who called me to go boldly beyond all the limits that had been placed on us. When I stepped up for that race it felt more palpable. An outside, not in lane four at the centre of the pool with all eyes on me but just a little to the side, where they expected me to be. It was just impressive that I was there, that's what I imagined they would say, a footnote in their parents' conversations with friends when they watched these all-white finals and me. With this swim I was going to make a statement, my body had already decided that for me, not only as an accomplished swimmer but as the Black woman – because that's what they'd called me – in one of the whitest sports in the world.

I touched the wall first. 30.11. I touched the wall 00.01 seconds ahead of the Canadian. Maybe her touchpad was off, maybe she'd made a mistake, but today it didn't matter. My smiling face mattered, my heavy bones, these heavy Black bones mattered. I had swum a perfect race before, this wasn't one, but it almost felt better. It was August 2009, and I was fifteen years old, and at the end of that season – only for a couple of months – I was ranked first in the world. Black people don't swim they said. Black people can't swim. Well, fuck you, I thought.

XIV

The weights gym was set up in the old assembly hall in the main building of the school. Allison took our weights sessions; as well as being the assistant coach, she was the house mistress at the boarding house – my supposed surrogate mother. She barked, 'We're going to the point of failure today.' My turn came soon: box jumps. Metal boxes with white-lacquered legs and a rubberised top for grip when your trainers landed on it. My genes made this easy and I jumped higher and higher, higher than most of the boys. Then, the box was up to my chin. 'Allison, I can't do it.' I turned to her after looking at the box for almost a minute. I genuinely meant I couldn't; it was a physical calculation, not that I didn't want to. 'Yes, you can! Come on, Chay, let's go, stop fannying around!' She was brusque, as always. 'No, I really can't do it, it's just too high,' I came back at her because I knew exactly how this would end, and I thought she should have known too, because so rarely did any of us ever say no. We said, 'Yes, Roan, of course, Roan, how high, Roan?' But this was too high. 'Jump!' she commanded. I inhaled, stepped back 30 centimetres. And just like before the 100-metre breaststroke, now the fear came down all around me. I stepped forward light on my toes, just about to jump, then I stopped myself. 'Allison, please, I really can't, it's too high.' The box stood at 1.4 metres; I was only 1.6. 'I'm not going to tell you again,' she said. 'Jump.' I jumped. The metal gashed through fascia to form white dents in my skin, so deep the blood came slowly as if through a sieve. 'Well, you talked yourself out of that one, didn't you?' she said. It felt accusatory. I looked up at her, bright red pools expanding slowly in the cotton of the top of my socks. I said nothing, because there was nothing to say. 'Again,' she instructed with no emotion.

This is what it takes.

I don't know when I'd started to question that. Was there a single moment I could point to before this? Not the broken pumps and the dead frogs ejected out of the freezing pools back in Cape Town. Not my burning feet on hot concrete, running to dip them in the water at the pool's edge for relief because there were no stands to shield me from Kenya's harsh equatorial sun. For months now I had felt Roan's hypervigilance, watching me almost every session, and I imagined he was looking at me greedily and whispering in my ear, 'They're all amateurs, it's you and me at trials, we're going to go boom, it's time for a big swim.' That's what he would say to me, bent down with his hand around the back of my neck, holding me still.

In reality Roan kept whispering to me, always making sure

everyone could see. That they could see that I was the most special trophy, shining twisted braids of muscle and a strong set jaw as he whispered. And I had taken to nodding, with my jaw that I'd clenched for so many years, set and unmoving. I used to do it for strength, in defiance, now I did it to stop the mangled sounds of dissociation escaping from my lips, to stop myself from saying I can't, I can't, I don't want to, I'm scared. I would fall asleep to his voice: 'It's time for a big swim, a big swim, it's time for a big swim.' I was voiceless, and even in my dreams I was nodding, but I was so small. This is what it takes. I knew then that a part of me would never stop believing it: something inside me, that had been there long before Roan had encouraged it to bloom. Roan had seen it in me, from the very first moment, and I knew this because I overheard him giving a comment for an article I'd been interviewed for. When I left the room and he took the phone back he said, 'We're only two years into this project. She hadn't had any real training when she came to us. Her times were nothing special when she arrived, but she was smart and she was hungry.' I could imagine him saying hungry; hungry like he had been over the years to find the exact spot inside me where shame reclined, lounging with the little girl who wanted to play her recorder so perfectly that people would love her and maybe her daddy wouldn't have left, and right there, that's where Roan lodged this belief. He lodged it so hard I knew it was never coming out. This is what it takes.

*

I slid my silver laptop out from under my bed, heavy and dappled with a mottled silver shell and an imprinted logo in the middle. On Facebook people were starting to send me messages, not a lot because it wasn't public knowledge yet, but back in Kenya, people were obviously talking, so every day they came. 'You're a traitor, you have no patriotism, Kenya needs you and you are leaving us!!' Some were more pleading: 'Why are you going, you are the best swimmer, we have looked up to you for many years since you swam at the pool near Lavington Green.' Then some were ugly and pure: 'How much money are they paying you to swim for them? Didn't think you could be bought.' I slammed my laptop lid closed, sinking into the space between the headboard and the wall that protected me from the door to my dorm room and the outside world and everything in it. I was falling inside myself and I was so close to shutting the door on it all. Listless, I fell, further and further away from the few moments I reached out to anyone. I was a shell, a husk of the person I had left somewhere in the season before. I knew she wasn't coming back and that I was never going back to her. The truth was, there was no money in swimming, not really, not unless you went to the Olympics and got on the podium, and with my change in sporting nationality, I had just given up my automatic spot at the Games. And what was I being promised in return? A chance to be the best. But I was already the best in some ways, though at the time that thought never occurred to me. My mum wanted me to go to the Olympics, and so did Roan and Julia, and all my old coaches, and Kenyan Swimming, all the people sending me messages on Facebook, the two brothers on the Kenyan team and their father, our old team manager, and now British Swimming as well. Nothing was as important as the Olympics; I knew that was what I was supposed to think. And I didn't think anything was more important, I just didn't think *anything* was very important anymore.

'What's wrong, babes?' It was James. We had moved through trepidation towards friendship slowly over the last season, his Plymouth twang comforting as he sat on the bench beside me. He was built like a Masai but with caramel skin like mine and broad African features with clever eyes. To me, he was the light amid my current darkness. Everyone said we looked the same so sometimes we pretended to be related. 'Don't hide from me,' he teased. 'Is it Allison being a cow?' I rubbed my hand down my thigh instinctively towards my shins in response. It wasn't the pain or how much it was going to sting in the harsh chlorine in our training session later. If anything, they were battle scars. Two small eyes halfway down the bottom of my legs looking out at everyone, daring them to take me on. It was doubt. So I asked James, 'Do you think I should do this nationality switch?' I looked ahead so he didn't see my glassy, despondent eyes, desperate for guidance. 'Chay, you've literally got nothing to lose, we literally have nothing, look at where we are,' he paused, gesturing to the tired playing fields in front of us and the grey that hung over our whole lives here. 'If you don't kill it at trials, it's going to be over anyway, how much longer have you really got?' He wasn't really asking, and I couldn't answer because we both knew that saying it out loud was dangerous, but I'm sure he felt me bristle beside him.

Our bench was just outside the weights gym, and in the cricket club across the vista I could see the boys in the year above getting ready for an away game, laughing and walking slowly and forgetting things and turning round. Their coach, the lower-sixth economics teacher, was waiting patiently by the door. 'I know,' I whispered back to James in response, my voice so small he softened. 'You've got this, and you're gonna take it all – otherwise,' he paused, 'otherwise you'll just be an African wild-card at the Olympics, and you'll go even if you don't get the qualifying time and what are you going to get back for that?' Still he went on: 'Get all the sponsorship, get a car, the Speedo deals, just get it all before you're all used up,' he finished. In a way, I knew he was right. We never lied to each other; we saw the world in exactly the same way, so what would have been the point? 'Are your knees okay from earlier?' I asked him. We were about to go to training, and he was a breaststroker like me, I knew he needed them. 'Babes, my knees are fucked, just like yours.' He laughed and got up and put his hand out; I took it reluctantly and let him pull me to my feet.

I walked slowly back over to the gym. Roan had taken the early session and he and Julia had crossed paths for the hand-over. I was about to carry on walking towards the entrance to the pool when I heard his voice lift and saw her turn around. I stopped myself just before I rounded the corner, just in time to hear Roan. 'I don't fucking want to hear it,' he said. He was snarling, but quietly. She responded by pushing her shoulders back as she looked up at him. They were arguing, or at least they were thinking about starting an argument. From my vantage point I only caught snippets, they were out of full earshot of anyone coming into or out of the gym, '. . . Write you out of the picture . . .' – that was Roan – 'I don't understand why you're . . .' Julia started, but I couldn't hear the rest of her sentence. If I had had parents who fought, I assumed this was how it would feel: me, an anxious and paralysed voyeur, and them, seemingly unaware of the mounting damage they were causing. Suddenly Roan turned. I watched as he finished apparently insulting her and moved to walk past her. Julia said something to his back, but he walked on to his car without turning round, his unseasonal khaki flip flops slapping lazily as he went. I was standing round the corner biting my nails down to the skin as I listened. And then, as if that weren't enough, I ripped my cuticles even further from their beds, taking more and more territory until the blood rushed forth and disrupted my view. I heard the beep of the car as it opened and watched Roan lower himself into a gleaming new BMW and drive off.

On poolside a couple of weeks later, with scabs on my shins and the promise of two matching concave scars, I stood prepping a second bottle with a sachet of SIS lemon electrolyte powder, early for training. 'A professional athlete, that's what I like to see!' Roan said in a loud sing-song voice as he came through the door at the top of the pool. A year ago, I would have cringed, embarrassed at being singled out as the rule following adult-pleaser I always had been, but there were only three other people on poolside and I also didn't care anymore. Roan would always tell this story about when I came to try out at Plymouth back in 2007. 'Effectively, I was being interviewed by a thirteen-year-old girl,' he would laugh with the other coaches on poolside at competitions. 'Yeah, yep, exactly, can you imagine, and she had a notebook full of questions as well!' He would go on, pleased with his audience and the crowd-pleasing story that I had heard over and over. 'You know, you only ever coach a few really professional people in your career. She had that at thirteen, an aura, so smart, so mature.' The story wasn't quite true; at least I didn't think so. I couldn't remember because it had been used so effectively to shape my personality. 'She's so smart,' I heard people say to my mother about me when I was younger. 'She's so bright, so independent.' My mother, who had made me like that, enjoyed hearing it even more than I had. But now I didn't know the truth. Was I smart? I was performing averagely at school, better when I paid attention and better still when I had the time or inclination to do my homework. 'So smart' seemed like a stretch. But every flight I took by myself, every solo train journey, every hotel room I'd sat in alone, every call room I'd bent to my will through sheer focus, my ability to control my nerves when no one else around me could – it all stood as evidence to the contrary. It felt to me now, though, that Roan had bent the truth with his insistence on my intellect, and then he hid the truth from me as he went on continuing to insist on it in all the interviews that he gave about me. I was so smart and so professional and so mature that I was about to change sporting nationalities at fifteen and I had made the decision all by myself, apparently. I was terrified all the time, and I couldn't sleep. But at least I was so smart.

XV

'Is someone going to tell her that her forehead is completely orange?' I looked at my roommate sarcastically. 'She looks nice and also I think that's how she wanted it.' She was putting bronzer on her own face as she replied, her peroxide-blonde hair almost cream-coloured and angelic; I felt mean for what I'd said. It was almost Christmas again and it was boiling hot. We were in Doha for the World Schools Championships, a big international competition where each country was represented by the best of their school-aged athletes.

A bus ride through sandy streets lined with gated houses took us to a mall which was a copy of a copy; Venice translated through Vegas had been built here in this brand-new shopping complex, a canal and gondolas followed us around under plastic bridges as we walked from the Nike outlet to the food court. The shops had yellow brick façades and Venetian windows on their top floors with an artificial amber glow behind them. The canal was a synthetic blue – with no sky to reflect, it took on the swimming-pool blue of its floor, with a delicate black metal railing that ruled its edges and old-fashioned streetlamps with baskets hanging from their arms holding real red carnations. The strangest part of Villaggio Mall was the Renaissance-style painted sky: soft, pale orange and pink clouds peppered a baby-blue abyss that hung too close overhead on a low ceiling. It took me a long while to work out that it was strange because it was unmoving. The pool was also brand new, like everything else here; all the surfaces smelled like electronic goods that had just had their protective plastic film peeled off. Between all of these new buildings were vast, empty spaces and we travelled along empty four-lane dual carriageways to get from one to another: hotel to pool, pool to hotel and back again. With your headphones in, facing your twenty-three teammates on the bus, sometimes the air-conditioning was the only reminder that you were somewhere else. At the mall I sat with the girls, none of them from Plymouth; my friends now were all from Newcastle Swimming Club, a group of girls who were pretty and funny and didn't seem to register jealousy. Partly because we didn't train together, or swim the same events, but also because I had given them the chance to like me, and they did.

'This isn't a negotiation.' It was the assistant coach for my team back in Plymouth. Somehow, she'd become the coach for this competition, the ISF World Schools Championships. It was all small and political, the better club you were at the more chance you had of coaching the national team, the higher the profile the coach at your club had, the more that chance increased. I hated that she was here, but there wasn't much I could do about it at this huge meet in the middle of nowhere on a far-off time zone. I was sulking in the swim-down pool. Ellie, my roommate, was sculling slowly next to me, her perfectly manicured nails catching my eye, her goggles sitting neatly on her perfect head. 'Chay, Chay, it will be fine, it will be fine,' she sang. 'You swam slow on purpose, you know that.' – 'I do know that,' I said. I wanted to say that I only had one good swim per competition now; that I had started to become terrified, terrified all the time. A fear so large I couldn't fit my mouth around it, let alone give it words. To bring to my swims what I had to bring to make them electric, I couldn't do that more than once. Also, I was so close to the world record. And I could feel it on the tip of everyone's lips when they asked me, 'feeling ready?' or 'how was the warm-up?' It was even in their gaze as I felt their eyes on me while I stretched on poolside. Instead, I smiled at her. 'I know, I just – Allison is so annoying,' is what I said instead. Junior events often get landed with less than experienced coaches – like Plymouth's assistant coach, in this case – because it's their chance to lead a team internationally and no one cares about the wellbeing of junior teams. We were guinea pigs: an experiment for successful execution, which meant successful racing. I pulled out of the 100-metre final – Roan would never have let me do it, but Roan wasn't here. In the 50-metre breaststroke I swam a 30.73. It was my best ever long course time and one of the best times in the world, and once again just under 0.5 seconds off the world record. I took the gold, they raised the flag and played the British national anthem because I went to a British school, and I raised my flowers above my head towards my team with my dark blue and crimson kit on – not quite the Team GB kit, but it was close. Dan won the 200-metre backstroke and there was something between us because of that. For the first time it seemed like he wanted to be close to me – I was a success and he had joined me somewhere in the upper echelons, happy to be welcomed in.

The 4 × 100 metre medley relay was on the last night. I had swum slow again in the heats that morning, but we'd scraped into the final. You were only really allowed to do that if you knew exactly how slow you could go and still place in the top eight. The three other girls were all nerves, and I didn't know why; we were in the outside lane with no real chance of moving into any medal position. There was no pressure on them either; they couldn't do much to change our fate, only I could do that. A medley relay isn't swum in the same order as the individual medley event. Because it's a relay, the backstrokers start, in the water, and lead out for 100-metre backstroke, then breaststroke follows, then butterfly, then freestyle. So, breaststroke is the second 100 metres, making it arguably the most crucial. There isn't huge variation between decent freestyle or fly swimmers: if you're good, you'll all be going around the same time, give or take a couple of milliseconds. But breaststroke can vary wildly. There were only a couple of girls in the world who could swim under 1.08 at that time. And I had pulled out of the individual 100-metre breaststroke so I didn't know how fast I could go in this relay tonight. I'd bullied Allison with implicit threats about my performance and what Roan would say if I swam a 1.10, but I was scared. Scared to race against the clock and find that I couldn't go under 1.08. I was scared to try. It was just me, lane four, the touchpad and the time ticking up, up, always up.

In a relay, unless you swim first your time doesn't technically count. This is because a relay start sees you fling your arms round and almost run from the back of the board to the front. You start moving when your teammate's head is between the last tile and the wall. Time it right and you get this flying start, but your feet can't leave the block until their hand touches the wall. It's an art, a skill, and also a trust exercise. You have to trust that they will keep swimming at the wall just as fast as they have been and that they won't take an extra stroke that you haven't accounted for. You keep your eyes trained on them down along your hands, you watch them from over the ends of your fingernails, following their head as if sighting a rifle, until you don't; as soon as they are in position you swing, step and dive. A good relay handover, just like on the track, can be exponential in increasing your chance of success, and every good handover sees your team improve its position, especially if other teams fumble. In Plymouth we practised them all the time.

Straight away we slipped back. By the time they were coming into the wall after the backstroke leg, we were down in sixth position by a fair amount, and France and Germany were way out in front. I trained in on her, settling my mind to a quiet slumber. Breathe, swing, step, run, push, fly. In the water, in the safety of the outside lane, no one could see me flying. I was ahead by the 50-metre mark: never look, never check, another turn. I had done this more times than I had done anything else, every session again and again, every day, for the last five years, so, without thinking, I turned once more. I wasn't rested, so I felt strong. Strong down the second length of the pool, where normally the lactic defeated me, now my endurance saved me, and we were going. Under the flags and towards the wall and I felt Chloe disappear overhead. I turned my head to the left to see the rest of the pool. Three metres of clear, perfect water, at least four seconds, an expanse of synthetic blue. We were going to win. A small miracle that, because of me, we were going to win. Before I got out, I clenched my fist against me and looked up the stands at my team. Then we were all behind the blocks, Chloe had held onto our lead and the three of us had our arms around each other, screaming at our anchor, Asha. Some of the other girls had gained on her a little but she was holding on. 'Go, Asha, push, push, push, swim!' we screamed, we screamed her all the way under the flags and all the way to the wall. Dan and the boys were hanging over the stands: all the coaches and the rest of the team, everyone was on their feet, it was close, but not close enough, because it was ours. It was ours and we were having it. From lane one, right up against the wall, we'd swum through the cascading waves that ripped outward from the middle of the pool and hit the wall then bounced back at you, we'd swum against not a chance in hell of placing. The best thing about relays is that it doesn't matter who the best is: when you win, with swimming being the solitary sport it is, there is truly no better feeling.

Chloe grabbed me and we jumped up and down. Euphoria engulfed our bodies, wrapping us up and pushing us together. Asha got out and put her fingers up to the camera, 'Number one!' she mouthed, as she pulled her cap off and the cameraman came in closer. We punched the air again and again and looked up at our team, 'Come on, girls!' Dan was swinging his top around over his head. I was the first to notice the scoreboard because it wasn't up high, built into the wall in the centre of the pool, it was right next to me, a large portable black block erected on the poolside floor, an electronic screen with dancing orange numbers and letters visible to 80 per cent of the stadium from its resting place. When a race finishes, the scoreboard shows everyone's times just as the race has been swum, in their lanes; then, a couple of seconds later it jumps into order and shows the times chronologically, the winners first, complete with FINA record codes: WR for world record, GR for games record, NR for national record and so on. The board was static, our time still in lane one, and at least two minutes had passed since the end of the race. We'd been disqualified, I knew it straight away and swallowed hard to accept it. Not because I didn't care, which I was later accused of, but because the moment was so painful I couldn't bear to put off processing it. The longer I pretended it wasn't happening or that we might appeal, the worse it felt. I looked at the girls, still celebrating behind me; in thirty seconds they would know too, but I let time drag on as I stood in the stadium, my heart falling down inside my suit, following the water that was running down to my ankles. Something was shifting inside me, and even though my experience carried me through that moment, something was lost at that pool after that swim that I didn't fully realise I was losing at the time. I had just swum a 1.06. That time would have put me on the podium at the previous Olympics, second to Leisel Jones; it would have put me on the podium in 2012 as well. Relay swims were always fast because of the flying start so for that reason it wouldn't be recorded, but if we hadn't been disqualified, I might have been able to hold onto it. It would be recorded somewhere, in a digital transcript of the event, in some archive, the possibility that I could swim that fast would be written down and enshrined forever. Instead, they would record the worst code there was: DNQ for disqualified.

We were all stuck, stuck in these moments forever. We were supposed to be winners, and when we weren't, it was as though you could see clearly that there wasn't anything else up ahead. Moments of defeat like this lifted the veil of hope. We'd all been duped, complicit in this delusion. Although she would go on to swim through her last year of school and on to a scholarship at a Division 2 college in America, Chloe's career ended that night. In the concrete stairwell, hysterical and hyper-ventilating with tears and shame, the other girls embraced her. 'It's okay,' they said, 'it happens.' I stood coldly in the corner. It wasn't okay. I had more moments, and my own gold medal from this competition already in my Speedo wheelie bag back in our hotel room, but Chloe had none. This was the highest peak she would ascend to and in failing to conquer it she would be scrap-heaped. As I prepared to keep climbing, I thought how great the fall would become when we'd ventured further up. I knew I would never forgive Chloe, not because she dived too early, but because she reminded us how perilous and precarious this journey was. And I felt jealous that she was beginning her journey back down already. The further to fall, the longer the ride, the harder I'd hit the bottom, far harder than this. Her ambition was curtailed now, her confidence destroyed, and in its destruction, she had taken some of mine as well. There would be no more attention for her, but also no more expectations.

At the hotel I followed Ellie and the Newcastle girls out onto the roof terrace. We were out past curfew, and they laughed as they spoke to the waiter and shook their hair and their spiky mascara-coated eyelash clumps at him. Here were girls who were growing up, who understood that you could get what you wanted by pushing your chest out. 'Can I try?' Ellie said in a high baby voice to the group of Arab men next to us. 'Sure.' The man looked at her and I think he saw a child as he slowly handed over the mouth of the roped pipe. The rest of the girls giggled. Ellie glanced at me, and I lowered my shoulders automatically. Her red nails reflected the low fluoro-lighting, she sucked her cheeks in dramatically, pursing her glossed lips around the plastic tube, and inhaled. I imagined the smoke filling my lungs, watched her chest rise and saw her diaphragm jump as she tried not to cough. She blew out, the plume dancing in the forbidden air between us.

XVI

County Championships came round once again, as they did at the beginning of every year. Each weekend the meet was held in a different part of Devon – strangely, never in the big cities, it was always Tiverton, or Weston-super-Mare, and always at old swimming baths or public pools. They all looked the same: an overcrowded poolside without enough seating and a mess of bags resting on the watery tiles, cubicle changing rooms and small gyms above the carpeted foyers. Always too much chlorine, an overpowering amount, and the pool was always too hot for fast racing. Depth and pool temperature are regulated at big international competitions; a shallow pool creates drag and resistance as waves form too easily and ricochet back up at the swimmers. And a hot pool dehydrates you. Fast pools are at least two metres deep and usually around 25.8°C. In these hot, shallow local pools across Devon, for the four weekends of January Roan instructed me to break the world record, the one

I had been 0.48 seconds away from at the Grand Prix at the end of the season before. I was to suit up and psych myself up week after week, with no regard for the context of the competition. County Championships was the bottom rung of swimming competitions; it was supposed to be a great encourager for swimmers starting out, with qualifying times accessible to those who only trained two or three times a week. Additionally, I was going to wear my sharkskin, while no one wore full racing suits like this at a County Championships. The humiliation was total.

He made me go for the record in every single event. This meant swimming the 200-metre breaststroke at a full sprint for the first 50 metres, touching the wall, not knowing if I'd broken the world record, and then having to turn and finish the race – that was the only way my time would count. Six excruciating lengths of breaststroke followed; you didn't flat-out sprint the first leg of 200 metres. I didn't break the world record. I got very close, every time, and because it was the beginning of the year, after every swim – heats then finals – every weekend for three weeks the commentator would say, 'Achieng Ajulu-Bushell, in a time of thirty point something something, and that's the third-fastest time in the world this year.' Then, 'That's the fifth-fastest time in the world this year', then 'That's the second-fastest time in the world this year'. Everyone looked on: bewildered parents, my teammates, full of judgement – did I think so much of myself, so important was I that I could take over this democratic gala with my world record-breaking agenda? It wasn't my agenda, but they were all my times and every weekend I told him, 'I can't break it here', and every weekend he commanded me to try again. I never broke the world record, and after County Championships that year it had been so sullied, and I had felt so stupid, that I didn't care about it anymore and I never thought about trying again.

*

'Everyone knows she's a little slut.' It was Dan, and he could have been saying it about any of the girls, they all said it all the time, but I knew who he was talking about. The rotation of relationships continued like clockwork; and the talk of sex continued in the boarding house, with rumours of the act continuing too. By the beginning of 2010, my third year at Plymouth, I was convinced that this was some kind of failing on my part, that I hadn't done it yet. I had got it into my head that I had to wait until I was sixteen, I think because it was the legal age, and it was still painful for me to break the rules, but also because I didn't grow up with boys who said 'slut'.

The boys carried on, 'She just doesn't know how to suck dick, not at all,' Dan was telling one of the boys. No one flinched. I believed that Jenkins didn't talk about me like this, but I wasn't certain – not that anything had really happened. I also knew that as soon as I did anything I would be the girl who didn't know how to suck dick, not at all. Ella, the new girl, who was a very young thirteen, sat frozen in front of me. She never wore make-up and called her mum all the time, her flat chest heaving when I saw her from the other end of the corridor; Ella reminded me of myself, and I quietly resented her for it. So precious and unknowing, she always said the wrong thing, always laughed too long, always tried so hard to be part of the conversation. We hit every red light on the fifteen-minute ride home from the main school to the boarding house that day and Dan didn't let up. I looked out of the window and watched the clouds rest heavy on the sooty buildings. Plymouth still held the scars of the war; roundabouts built around bombed-out churches and stained houses, black with coal and aged ash. A city mistreated, just like our bodies in the pool and in the gym and the bodies of the girls having underage sex in tiny single beds after lights out, their parents often hundreds of miles away.

If I was waiting until sixteen because that was the law, I was also waiting because I didn't think anyone wanted to sleep with the Black girl. It would be another two years until I started to realise what I looked like. I told myself I didn't want to do it yet, I wanted to wait until I was ready, but I was also scared that no one wanted to do it with me. I'm mixed-race, I'd always insist whenever the topic arose; I'm half white, I'd say, the words like a poison I was feeding myself. But the word Black stung too. It wasn't me, because I thought it just described a colour of skin and I wasn't that either.

I lost my virginity later that year, when I was sixteen, watching *Avatar* with the nicest boy in the world. He was two years older than me, and he was the kindest person I'd ever known. His life had been hard in different ways from mine, but I only ever hung out with boys who reminded me of my past, with working-class parents and straightforward childhood trauma. It felt uncomplicated to me; there was no judgemental family to impress, no expectation that I would be blonde or know the right thing to say. And they told me that I was hot, that they loved me, that I was funny; and I did their homework. My mum found the pill in the zip-up front pocket of my swimming bag one late afternoon training when she was visiting me in Plymouth. It had already long happened, but she was horrified. I cried as she tried to tell me how shocked she was at me, but only because I didn't understand her reaction. Among a thousand broken promises from everyone around me who'd said, 'We will protect you, and we'll keep you safe,' I had kept this one to myself. My mum could only see the broken promises of the people she'd entrusted me to, and the school nurse who'd given me contraception without informing anyone else. But I was proud of that act, my independence, and I refused to be swayed.

Trials loomed and taper finally came: training frequency and mileage decreased, we ate less because we were burning fewer calories and each day we woke up hungry and wondering if it would work. We were going back to Sheffield, but this time in March and only with a small handful of the team. British Championships were held a week after my birthday that year and it was there that they would select the British team for the European Championships later that summer and the England team for the Commonwealth Games in the autumn. I didn't feel Roan knew how to train me anymore. Julia and I were so deep in the nuances of every component of my technique that there was no room for anyone else. She was a breaststroke specialist, and we broke down every microsecond, every extension, every flexed foot and hyperextending elbow, every phase of my catch, each movement in the underwater pull-out after the dive. She knew how many strokes was good and how many bad. She knew what time my stroke rate would result in, and she made me guess my splits over and over until I knew just by feeling exactly what time I had swum, down to the split second.

As we continued to taper down, the volume of our sets decreasing and my time with Roan decreasing with it, I felt a shadow of my former self return. My dives became powerful and innate, like those of the girl back in Cape Town, brimming with raw talent and untarnished drive. Instead of the near-constant paralysing fear, I was able to feel the water again. I felt my body on the blocks poised and ready, rocking forward and pulling my head down just enough, then checking to see how it felt before readjusting my back foot by 3 centimetres and moving my head down another 7 degrees. This was a swimmer I knew. Julia smiled at me and held her stopwatch to her chest, beaming. 'Guess!' she said. I stood up in the shallow water at the far end of the pool, playful and smiling back at her, 'Erm, 13.76,' I said quickly. 'Ah!' She held the stopwatch out and down to me proudly. '13.59!' she almost squealed. I shrugged my shoulders forward in a shy way and smiled down at the tiles. This was fast swimming.

The boys, who were all racing at 1.06 – the same time as the fastest women in the world that year – couldn't keep up with me as the sprint sets progressed. No one wanted to say it, and least of all me, but this was it. Maybe I'd started to believe again, maybe that was what it took; the fear, the doubt, it was just a blip and I'd needed that to get to this point. Outside, the season turned in the windows of the pool and Roan and I found a new closeness, as if he was also acknowledging the dark winter where I'd lost my way and it had been hard, but it was all for this, and he had known all along that I would come out of it better and stronger than ever. Although I didn't think he understood the technical workings of breaststroke like Julia, he could see the outcome, and he understood what the numbers on the stopwatch could mean for him. We were never as close as in those weeks leading up to trials, even the relationship between him and Julia seemed better. We did our last 10 × 50 metres set and I was on top of the world. I led out in a 31.00 and didn't drop below a 35.5 even after throwing up twice and almost falling instead of diving in for the last two sets.

*

As soon as we got to the Holiday Inn, I watched a gnawing feeling squat and settle in the corner of the lobby. We walked from the main reception up the wide carpeted staircase as we'd always done, and I could feel my stomach softly churn: PRD, we called it, pre-race-diarrs, the anxiety and the cortisol liquefied everything inside you. Some people threw up before races, but with most it came out the other end. Kayli and I were sharing a large room on a different side of the hotel from usual, with two double beds and a big TV. Over the weekend I woke up each day to patterned curtains and the feeling that I was small again, back at my grandma's house, which was covered in dog hair and packets of stamps. My mum was only ten years older than I was now when she had me and the curtains in her bedroom had had this same lifeless pattern. I was trying to tell myself something, but by the time I became aware of it I was already too awake, and I'd remembered where I was. The only words I was left with were 'go back'. I'd start each day with this unsettling feeling, that I needed to 'go back', to when, I didn't know, just a time before. After training that Sunday, in the large 50-metre pool that I now knew so well, I walked up the hill with the tram line on my right past Greggs and into town where the roads flattened out. I wandered into M&S while on the phone to my mum, talking about the order of the races that week and who was there but also letting her talk me into a trance with all the research she'd done. This was our ritual: she would call, and we would talk only about the competition and the history of my competitors: who'd posted what times this season and how people had been racing coming into trials. This was our way of preparing, recovering a sense of control to soothe my nerves by not acknowledging my nerves at all.

I was near the check-out as I moved the phone absentmindedly from my left hand to the cradle between my right ear and my shoulder and reached down to the Sunday paper that was sitting on the rack in front of me, 'Swimming' and 'Sheffield' in the top banner of the front page had caught my eye. I turned it over, and when I saw the picture on the back page, I knew the last few weeks had been a mirage and that my unburdened mind had just been a journey through a porthole to nowhere. If time and space could be bent, then it had been, and I had touched some previous version of myself, but only in passing, on my way to here. I had been treating swimming the way I wanted it to be, with no stakes. But the black-tiled floor of the shop absorbed that reality, which disappeared in an instant as I stood there. All the levers that had been pulled silently in the background, the quick phone calls Roan would always make while observing me, and the men that I was constantly meeting with small notebooks in their big hands, who wanted to know what I thought about schoolwork and being Kenyan. Behind the scenes it had all been working towards something else, something bigger than I could have known, and in that moment, I knew it was going to happen all at once. In full colour, the picture took up two-thirds of the page. My mouth was contorted and huge, flanked by even bigger shoulders, my hands in prayer cresting out of the water, dark scars of old hyperpigmented spots visible in blurred pixels on my forehead in the small space just between my swimming cap and my eyebrows. The mirrored silver lenses of my goggles reflected the wall on the other side of the pool, two tiny images of the empty lane that had stretched before me were contained in those discs over my eyes, seeming to say, 'There's nothing up ahead, go back.' The shop was silent, and my phone had fallen to the floor.

Race

XVII

'No I will make no peace
Even though my hands are empty
I will talk as big as I please
I will be all or nothing'

Mohja Kahf

The article went live on the 30th of March 2010 and unlike the lite replications that followed, it presented itself as a detailed exposé, twisting facts into a bombastic examination. Kenyan runners changing sporting nationalities so they could 'live lavish lifestyles in the Middle East'. Apparently, according to the article, when I'd been asked, I hadn't wanted to dwell on any 'awkward questions' about my reasons for changing sporting nationality. 'Loyalty to one's country of birth is becoming an ever more tenuous notion.' The line stuck out to me, and I read it over and over. Why were they so obsessed with immigrants? Somehow this was what the article had to dredge up. I had no memory of the supposed 'awkward questions' because all the questions were awkward. National allegiance. Patriotism. Flags of sporting convenience. This decision was my birthright which, although acknowledged, sat pathetically small and low down on the page, and these accusations were only 'largely unfair' according to the article, suggesting that they weren't completely unfair – because who was I, to come over here with my Black skin and complicated background and also happening to be very good at swimming?

I had just become British Champion for the first time, winning the 50-metre breaststroke by a whole second. It wasn't really a competition, but my time wasn't where I wanted it to be. Nothing about my taper had transformed the way my body felt. I read the article again. I was so strung out and on edge since finding it the day before trials started, my psychological state weakened to a point so fragile I could barely be around other people at all. Julia was trying to help me – I could see that – she would come and sit with me on poolside before I went over to the call room, trying to get there before Roan. But Roan behaved towards her the way he did to everyone else, and the media train had already left the station. The thing that surprised me the most was the fact that no one had told me this was going to happen, and because of that it was impossible to interrogate. As if it could be anything other than normal, a natural progression of my training and my young life in this mini high-performance centre that Roan had built around me. 'Ajulu-Bushell to become first Black woman to swim for Great

Britain.' My career had a life of its own now, with little awareness of my near-constant state of anxiety.

'Ajulu-Bushell, a World Schools swimming champion last
year, will become the first Black woman ever to swim for
England and Britain if things go to plan at trials in Sheffield
this week. In her sights: a "home" London 2012 Olympic
Games.' The violence of the inverted commas hung around the
word I knew better than anyone. What did this journalist know
about home? The casual way other people used it, he probably
did the same: 'I'm going home' they'd say, 'I'll see you at home',
or 'I can't wait to get home'. I didn't know when I was going
to get home, I never had. Home was my mother, and home
was also something I'd thought about my whole life, a question
that for most was so straightforward but for me never had an
answer that came to an end. A home Olympics. Did he mean
this wasn't my home? Yes, of course, but also that it *could* be.
I didn't know what I had to do in order for that to be true. In
all the places I had lived and left and called home, and in all
the people I had loved who'd left so I could no longer call them
home, the answer had always evaded me. What did I have to
do to stay in one place and have them stay with me? When I
was old enough to realise it, I knew home was a place that
would never be fully mine. After growing up in Nairobi and
then returning there in the many years since I'd left, I'd grasped
more and more how much my lighter skin made me stand out.
Sometimes, when we'd drive up-country and pass a village, I
would see children walking home from school and they'd point
and scream 'Mzungu! Mzungu!' – in Swahili it has come to

mean 'white person'. And I would always think, 'Where, who is the white person?' Until I realised they meant me. The literal translation of mzungu, though, means 'someone who roams around endlessly' or 'aimless wanderer'. Being half Kenyan, half British means that one half of me colonised the other. And since I grew up between these two places and with that violence inside me everywhere I go, it also means that home is neither here nor there and the wanderer is who I am.

Even though I was born in Warrington, for years now I'd said Manchester because even as an outsider I knew something about class without ever being told. 'The sixteen-year-old is a member of a family with some weighty players in the world of African politics, and a best pal and classmate of world champion diver Tom Daley at Plymouth College,' the article read. That was kind of true, but the way it was written made it seem like I was someone else. Tom and I were friends, sure, but also we just trained all the time, and not together. And my father was politically connected, now at least, but the text hinted at something almost sinister about it. My line, or the line I was supposed to take, sounded so pleading when I read it back: 'I was born here. I have a British passport; my mum is English.' I didn't realise how humiliating it would all feel when it was written down for me to read, but the humiliation was twofold; it was worse because I'd wanted to say it. It went on: 'Kenya will wake up to news of the swimmer's decision in the morning – and headlines will follow on a girl who has appeared on the cover of teen and women's magazines and is linked to some of Africa's biggest political players: her father, Rok Ajulu, a leading African politics professor and son of Stephen Odero Ajulu (a leading political activist in the 1960s in the Kenya People's Union) is married to Lindiwe Sisulu, South African defence minister. The daughter of freedom fighters Walter and Albertina Sisulu, she was arrested and faced a life sentence at the age of twenty-four at a time when she served as an intelligence officer for the African National Congress. Now, Sisulu is a potential first woman president of her country, some pundits suggest.'

Who was this person? I didn't know her. As for Lindiwe – I'd never met her but I imagined how much she would hate the fact that we were all here together on the page and unable to escape the messiness of imperfect choices. I'd been mostly invisible, out of her orbit and largely out of my dad's life, until now. There were so many people in the frame, so many eyes to evade and so much to manage. My mum's voice also danced along in the paragraph below, 'She does not stop being Kenyan. That will always be a significant part of her, and she will always be tremendously grateful for what Kenya has given her. It was a very difficult decision and an absolutely huge gamble. She has sacrificed an automatic place at the Commonwealth Games, Olympic Games and given away the World Youth Olympics because Britain isn't going. But she gambled all of that for something she really believes in . . .' I'd believed in my body once, and that I could do what no one else could, but I could hear its scaffolding rattling now, vibrating against a weight that was bearing down into the centre of the earth.

'Expect the delightful and confident Ajulu-Bushell to win

hearts and minds,' the journalist wrote. It felt like he was talking about a biopic of my life that was about to be released this week at the Sheffield Ponds Forge pool to throngs of critics holding mouldy fruit. But the film would prevail, winning over the sceptical masses who would take their fruit home instead of throwing it. 'What a nice exotic girl,' they'd say in the taxi back. Ostensibly, I had been made ready for this moment, but I don't think I could ever really have been ready for the moment I became Black in print. On Portobello Road, during carnival weekend, there was a small stand that sold children's books with little brown girls in African stories and names people couldn't pronounce, just like mine. I had let myself become 'Chay' on poolside, and in the classroom, divorced from the score board that spelled out A-c-h-i-e-n-g after every race, I would soon trade it in for Rebecca. My legal first name in the passport I was always shouting about. Because I'd grown up in Kenya, no one had ever called me anything other than my second name, Achieng, until I heard someone shout 'Becky' in the courtyard that first year at Plymouth. I took half of everything from each of my parents. My first and second names from my mother and father respectively, and then my surname from them both. Mixed and in-between, half this and half the other, but never Black. 'While she would not want to be singled out because she is Black,' my mother had been quoted, 'she is aware that she has a potential platform to break down barriers and challenge stereotypes that are simply wrong, like "Blacks don't swim". She is very aware of her ability to be a role model as an African and a Black athlete. If she were to get the opportunity to represent England at the Commonwealth Games, one of the challenges will be to change the perception of Black swimmers. She's a role model in Kenya and we hope she will continue to be a role model to younger swimmers, Black British swimmers, and those across the world.' My mother loved me with her strongest heartbeats, she loved my coarse hair at the back that she learned to soften with pink cream and braid for me when I was three or four, she loved the cracked skin on my shins that turned grey in the Mombasa sun, a little brown bear, her beautiful girl, mixed-race with big perfect eyes; I don't think I had ever heard my mother call me Black.

*

As a breaststroke sprinter the 50-metre was my domain, but the 100-metre event was the only Olympic distance. In order to complete this transition and secure my spot in Great Britain's senior team to represent my other country at the international events of the season and beyond, I had to serve an obligatory year out of international competition – which I had just done – and then I had to win the 100-metre event at the end of this week's trials. My time on Tuesday for the 50-metre put me second in the world this year, just behind Leisel Jones. Microphones had met me out of the pool and being out of breath had helped me to hide my bitter disappointment. It wasn't a big swim for me, not even close: at least 0.3 slower than in Doha three months before. The man from the rooftop in Rome who I now knew to be the Director of British Swimming was interviewed shortly after. It was a 'world-class swim,' he said. 'The biggest challenge, beyond this, is to clear her to swim for us at London 2012: under Olympic rules it is the Kenyan Olympic Association that must grant permission of transfer, not the swim federations domestic and international.' His tight, stretched face pulled slowly around the word Kenyan. 'It's hard to imagine,' he went on, 'any nation flying in the face of an Olympic charter that holds the athlete's wishes paramount. Very few would begrudge any athlete who soared as high as flying the Union Flag at a home Games the right to also acknowledge the other half of their heritage.' I wondered if they would have let me go so easily, and made so much of the fact that they should, if it had been the other way around.

Back at the hotel, Roan was giving another interview in the atrium room beyond the reception. I loitered at the door, even though he'd told me to come in, and listened to him as he moved his arms like a conductor and performed for me in front the journalist. 'At that time, her times on paper weren't particularly special.' I'd heard this once before, but it was wounding nonetheless. He went on: 'It was the individual sat before us who was special. It was her personality and her forthrightness and a clear intent about what she wanted to do in the sport, linked to the fact that she had a limited training background.' When Roan said things, they became true to everyone, and especially to me. He pushed his chair back and leaned further into the story. 'There was so much more that we could give her and add to – that's why we took her,' he carried on. 'She was very exciting to all of us.' I knew this part of the story by heart now. 'She opened up her notebook and I saw the long list of questions. She's now sixteen going on twenty-one. And she was thirteen going on twenty-one then. She's very confident, very mature, nothing arrogant, nothing unpleasant about any of that. It was just someone who was so keen on getting it right.' That made me sound pretty pathetic, I acknowledged now: how easily I'd fallen under the spell of putting swimming first, everything else a distant second. Roan was deep into the concert, so much so that I could feel the exact moment he was about to overplay his hand. 'There's a family feel to the coaching staff around her and indeed the whole team,' he began matter-of-factly. 'It's first-class care, like living 24/7 on a training camp. That atmosphere is very conducive to success. It has the feel-good factor.' No comment, I thought. 'I lead a very talented coaching team, at least 50 per cent of the work she does is with Julia, my assistant coach, and also Julia and I have built different relationships with Achieng.' He had the wind behind him now. 'The swimmers' strength and conditioning coach, Allison, is also her house mistress and surrogate mother at Plymouth College.' I almost laughed out loud. 'There is even a sports psychologist on call, as well as a performance analysis manager,' he remarked. The journalist spoke for the first time since the interview began. 'It's like a mini intensive training centre?' he ventured. 'Yes, you could say that . . . that's what we've got,' Roan replied. 'We even have biomechanical expertise and—' He broke off, and I thought he might be about to walk some of it back before I saw the vein on the left side of his neck. He was going to deliver the pièce de résistance: 'The beauty of her finally being British is that we can now extend the expertise of the British sports science and medicine team and the world-class development programme . . . now we can tap into that, the funding and the visibility, and really see what we can do.' There it was – his true ambition laid bare for all to see.

*

'Why are you always just watching weirdly?' I remembered Sara saying to me once in the boarding house. 'Like what?' I'd replied. 'Like a creep,' she'd said. It was half true. I did watch, I had to; certain I was still an imposter and I would make a mistake and make it known if I wasn't vigilant, I watched to see how they talked, how they wore their jeans at the weekend, what the boys responded to, what they said about girls with short hair and curvy bodies. I was always watching, trying to cleave some power out of fitting in. Because I was always watching, I never fully looked at myself. I was too busy imagining how close I could get myself to being like them. I knew that beauty was a weapon: it was power, just like success. The boys made our sport the synthesis of these two things, half-naked perfect forms and perfect forms that won. The girls had to choose, but I didn't feel like I'd ever had a choice; the athleticism of my body was pronounced before I could ever have decided I might want it soft and beautiful. I was built for success, for winning, and now the positions were reversed; everyone was watching me. I didn't know if they wanted to see me win – maybe they did, but this week, I wasn't going to let them decide. Through gritted teeth and blinkers, again by a clear second, I won the final of the 100-metre breaststroke on the penultimate day of the Championships. It was my race. On the podium I thought about the article again. It had finished with a final line about my parents, 'She is the daughter of a Black Kenyan father exiled at the height of the Moi repression and a white English mother. Much will be made of it.' The gold medal hung lightly around my strong neck, around the deep brown colour and fast twitch muscles my father gave me, and the resilience and belief my mother laid down in my bones. No one was going to make more of it than me. Because I'd just made history.

XVIII

It's always the people who know the least about sport who have the most to say. That starts with journalists and ends with beer-soaked men in pubs talking about the angle of the ball or the dart that didn't meet its target. Before I was British Champion, I'd existed as pure id. I had exorcised my ego so that it lived outside my body, and had for many years. This meant I didn't care if I lost. Every time I stepped up to win a race I was prepared for the outside possibility of loss, that it might not go my way, and it was exactly that vulnerability that made me a winner. But when my brown skin came into contact with the water that week in Sheffield, it no longer felt like returning humbly to my home. While others continued undisturbed, I started to sink under the racist mythologies of my sport. Then the media, along with Roan and British Swimming and a hundred other stakeholders – in an arena that wasn't built for someone like me – made me reingest my ego. And I became so scared of losing, it was all I could do to stand behind the blocks without my knees buckling. I let a dissociated malaise take me out of myself and somewhere else: away from that lane, and that heat and that race, somewhere that didn't make me feel like such a hopeless failure before the scoreboard confirmed it. I'll tell you about the hellscape that followed, but before I tell you about that, I'm going to tell you about professional swimming and elite sport, about anything carnal and repetitive.

Swimming looks simple: not physically, but as a sport. Just a pool with people floating in it, trying to go fast. It doesn't show you the impossibility of the discipline, because most people don't have any frame of reference for how fast they can swim. That's why it doesn't have the same following as tennis or track and field. But swimming is almost the purest expression of sport. You use nearly every muscle in your body, it's one of the few sports that does, and you're always moving forward as fast as you can, trying to get to the other side first. They would have you believe that there are more complex forces at play, or more shared desires, but swimming is only ever about trying to be better than you were last season, or last week; better than yesterday, or the you in your last session. It's about only you, and a limit you hope doesn't exist, a private dream of immortality: the deepest desire of all. If you do anything enough, it turns out like this: you are the only constant, and it ceases to be about anything else. If you do something for five hours a day, every day, for years, and you have coaches telling you how to do it, helping you improve incrementally, and that improvement becomes so incremental that you're chasing 0.4 of a second, or perfect form, or something like nirvana, it doesn't matter if it's swimming or football or even financial trading or playing the flute; you're there for its own sake. And that is what sport is: sport is completely pointless in every way. If you can do a thousand keepie-uppies with a football or run up a mountain faster than anyone else, it's ultimately all for the pure doing of the act, for the intensity of the experience, the thrill of the game. And that is the best and most important thing about it.

The birth of professional sport has of course perverted its nature. In order to win consistently, you have to not care about losing, but when you're competing professionally, the only thing that really matters is that you win. Professional sport is not the Olympics: professional sport is corruption and greed; it's forced doping and unequal resource allocation; it's governing bodies and bribes and eyewatering advertising contracts. And professional sport is coaches – with a throng of used-up athletes in their wake – being elevated from the heat of poolside and the exhaustion of morning training into an air-conditioned office and a job with consulting hours, and then a bigger office filled with engraved glass awards and finally a conference halfway around the world and a seat at a big table in a boardroom. Professional sport is not for the thrill of the game. Because, as I was learning, in professional sport, people have to explain why they've lost. They're made to publicly list all the reasons; but the reasons for losing never matter, least of all to a winner. And very soon I knew that I was going to have to say, 'This is why I lost,' or that people would start saying it for me. The battle, then, is to enter this arena that cares mostly about the outcome and attempt to stay focused on the process and the beautiful pointlessness of it. I didn't know any of this; I didn't know what I was getting into with British Swimming or what I was letting go of when I left Kenyan Swimming behind. But I did know that in swimming, just like in all sport, and in life, there is no balance, no cosmic justice, no deserving. Simply: sometimes it's your turn, and sometimes it's not.

There are lots of different ways to be a winning athlete. I wasn't the tallest or the strongest and I didn't have a special technique, something that I was doing that no one else was. A lot of people get by on pure talent, or physiology, sometimes sheer training; I always had the edge psychologically. If you want to do anything well, the most dynamic way of fuelling yourself is to feel close to survival: the primordial motivator of our lives. Every intrusive thought is about being alive. In the water, I got a taste of this intensity, and I loved it, and so I'd ask myself, every race: 'How am I going to maximise my heightened state?' And when you do this enough, the act of doing it can take on a life of its own, just like the perfect race, when I was more alive than I'd ever been. Then the only way to keep doing it is to tell yourself that you're different, you're special, and everything you do, think and feel is different from anything that anyone else can do and think and feel. You're closer to the void and you've been closer to it than anyone else would dare to go, and you know what might be beyond it too. And if you keep going, just a little faster, a little harder, a little more, you'll be standing at the edge of the world all alone and then you'll be able to reach out and touch it. Sport is also about being alive.

When I was fourteen, there was a girl who would go on to win a medal at the Olympics and I competed against her in her event: 200 metres individual medley, one length of each stroke, starting with butterfly. I was not good at any distance further than 100 metres, nor at butterfly, and I definitely shouldn't have beaten her, but I did. I remember that being the first time I realised that you could beat people who were truly better than you. 'If I touch before her on the first length, she will crumble,' I'd thought, and I was right. Because the problem with 'good' is that it has no strategy. You think good wins, you think, 'I'm going to be the best, so I'll win,' but that's not a strategy, that's just being good and trying hard. Strategy is in the process, in your survival instincts, your will to disrupt, in your ability to hold your dreams at arm's length and out of view; it's to be obsessed with the process and not really think about the outcome at all. For all of these reasons athletes don't have any real relationship to non-athletes, and for all our proximity and physical exposure, swimmers don't have much relationship to each other either, and winners don't have much relationship to anybody. And Black girls who have just won British Championships don't have a relationship to anyone at all. I had been alone before, because I'd wanted to be the best, but I was alone in a new way now, because I was a winner. It's not that the relationships in my life didn't matter – my longing for my mother, the desire I'd held for Jenkins it was just that they weren't part of the tool set I needed to thrust forward to greatness; in my story of sport, they were fleeting characters. This is specific to a high-performance mentality: a lot of people who are very good at sport won't have become so for any reason other than the need to push themselves beyond what they think they might be capable of, again and again. They may say retrospectively, or when pressed, that the intimate and familial relationships in their life inspire them, but that's not really true – not in the race, not on the pitch, not in the moment. I watched a tennis player almost beat one of the greats and in the interview afterwards he said, 'I thought about my parents,' and I thought, 'Big mistake, you're not going to win if you're thinking about your parents'. You can be very good at your sport, the best even, but are you also going to be the person who wins? Enduring winners have strategies that are diametrically opposed to the idea of being good. There are of course those chosen few who are just better. Contrary to what people believed, contrary to the myth I'd allowed to grow around me, I was not one of them. I was just an athlete who had learned to perform without ego. I loved the process; I loved the fear and I had it in abundance because I wanted to feel something bigger than any podium.

The world of sport is built like every great institution: with the power structures baked in. I was about to move into an arena that I didn't understand at all, an arena that's not well understood by anyone outside of it because the fallacy of professional sport is that it's not the world of work. It is, only about a thousand times more heightened. And it comes with everything you can imagine, except the output is realised through your body, not a computer. I was owned now; although I didn't fully know it, I had suspected it for some time. I was owned by people I knew very well, and I was owned by people I didn't know at all. I was even owned by history. But the weight of my Blackness I owned alone. When the dust settled on the British Championships in 2010, I was British Swimming's Olympic breaststroke hopeful; I qualified for the European Championships later that summer, and in the autumn, to swim for England at the Commonwealth Games. I also qualified to represent the hopes of those bound to an enduring mythology that said people like us can't swim. The interviews and the interrogation of the colour of my skin did much to bind me to the immensity of this pressure: 'You're going to be the first,' they said, and then they'd ask me how I felt about it. How did I feel? I felt like everything I'd loved about this sport was no longer accessible to me, the process was no longer my concern, and everything I thought about the void and what might be beyond it couldn't matter anymore. No one wanted me to experience the sheer delight of challenging myself and being alive and being in love with the water. They wanted me to prove them all wrong, and because I'd already won so much, they wanted me to prove them wrong while winning.

XIX

We were children. That's what it said in the *Times* article. Ever since British trials there had been a steady stream of articles applauding Roan and the partnership between our school and his club. An 'unsung hero' one called him; another wrote that his programme had won plaudits from the head of Russian Swimming. It described Plymouth, Roan's Plymouth, as a parallel to the other centres for sporting excellence, senior swimming programmes across the country that were working towards glory at a home Olympic Games, but his was for children of school age. I read the article from the pine desk in my room on my heavy laptop. My new roommate was lying on her bed, which she seemed to do whenever I was around. 'Are you going to revise?' I asked her without looking up. 'Not right now,' she replied slowly in her heavy south-eastern-European accent. Our exam was tomorrow and lights out was less than two hours away. I shrugged at her, and this time lifted my eyes from the screen.

Her single bed sat against a radiator under a big bay window that slid open from the top and the bottom. A pale green checked duvet cover sat on top of a cornflower bed sheet that was pulled too tight and puckered, like my fake cotton school shirt that was mostly viscose and pulled over my broad back and big shoulders, and like our bedclothes, smelled of chlorine. 'Aren't you scared of failing?' I couldn't help but probe; it was so improbable to me that she wouldn't feel the mounting pressure, or that no one was putting it on her. The night before, we had had journalists in our room, asking me questions about the forthcoming Summer Championships. I had slipped away to message my mum; I was in meltdown because my French oral exam was in the morning, and it was almost 9 p.m. Mum, enraged, had called Allison, who eventually came into our room and told the journalists they had to leave, and my revision had resumed. We were just about to sit our final few GCSE exams. Spring had become summer, and I was racing towards my first senior international competition, my British Swimming debut. But first, I had what I would come to know as my last Nationals.

A storm was brewing; I could smell it, and I was wondering when I would feel the first raindrop. I walked to training that evening with Amelia trailing behind me. We'd become kind of friends again, and now we were exhausted from a day spent in the large assembly hall in silence, writing three exams almost back-to-back. Up ahead, I could see Julia walking out of the sports centre – she had taken to leaving as soon as the session finished and arriving only a couple of minutes before it started so she didn't have to cross paths with Roan on his way into or out of the late or early evening training. They only spoke when they were both on poolside and they were talking about swimming.

'Do you think there have been any more developments?' I asked Amelia in a low voice over my shoulder. She caught up to me – 'I don't know, this whole thing is bat shit' – and also lowered her tone. Julia saw us as she stopped to get her car keys out. 'Girls, girls,' she said quickly, ushering us to her. Amelia and I hated the situation as we saw it. But as much as we hated it, I would be pulled back in by Roan's favouritism, the warm glow I felt at being his chosen champion, because he loved me, because he loved what I'd done for his club. I did feel caught between them, and I don't know why I didn't tell anyone at the time; I don't know why Amelia didn't tell anyone either. We would stand with Julia outside the pool, hiding around the corner as she and Roan swapped over. Today she caught us on the tail-end of her session before his started, but sometimes it would be just after she'd finished coaching us. We supported her as she had supported us tirelessly for years, and we were happy to do it. Each day we'd pick up the thread of their relationship, which didn't seem to be getting any better. We could smell her nervousness and we felt it too, whispering just off pool deck.

After our exams, as the school cleared out and emptied, we carried on training. This was always when things were the most feral. Reality wasn't tangible; there was no first period, or homework, or revision, there was only the pool, Roan's rules, and the bubble; we sank into its centre and its filmy edge felt even more impermeable. A new girl had joined us that summer, young, with broken English and bright hair. Amelia and I tried to school her every breaststroke set. She was fast, and Roan liked the competition. I was unsettled: as the Europeans drew closer the articles came thick and fast. Pictures of me next to Tom in maths: 'Classmates with an Olympic Golden Dream' the headline read. 'Did you really google the Olympic stadium like you said in the interview?' Sara had asked me off-hand on the bus home. It was three days before we were due to leave for Sheffield for the Nationals once again, then I would go straight on to Budapest for the Europeans. 'No, of course I didn't look it up, it's just what you say in interviews,' I snapped back. I had looked it up. 'Good,' she said. 'Because you sounded like a loser.' 'It's going to be an amazing time,' I'd been quoted as saying. 'We're going to make people really proud.' I got off the bus and walked into the changing rooms with small tears collecting on the neck of my dark blue hoodie. I'd pulled the front of it up over my nose to hide my shame and my pride, and my crying face.

The girls were all talking about going down to the boys' corridor later that evening. The fire escape door was open, which it always was. It led to the metal stairs that ran down the back of the building and picked up the door at the end of the boys' floor, which was always left open too. The term before, one of the girls had accused a boy of forcing her to give him a blowjob. Conversation quickly turned to the question of truth. 'It wasn't,' some insisted, 'at least not in the way that they said.' But how could it not be true either? It was as true as consent could allow for two children, and it was as true as the shame she'd felt at the word 'slag' that had been permanently attached to her chlorine-damaged hair in the weeks that followed. And it was also as true as some of the boys saying he was a legend. He left the boarding house and the school soon after, and we understood we were not to tell anyone about it, meaning, of course, our parents. Swimming is an arena of open secrets, in the places where it's bad, everyone knows what's going on, or at least they know enough about the trauma and abuse that athletes are subjected to, or the lack of care and protection they receive, but no one is incentivised to speak out, least of all the athletes themselves. And institutions that close themselves off from reality in impermeable bubbles – that make their own rules, birthed from their made-up power structures – forget the normal rules of a safe society. Often, in these places, rife with sexualisation, everything is lost because it can be.

*

A chipped tarmac car park doubled as a driveway. There were only a couple of parking spaces and then the concrete flagstones delineated a small patio area at the front entrance of the halls. Inside, thin carpet, pebbledash wallpaper and damp competed to cover every surface. We walked up the stairs to the third floor, careful not to touch the silver handrail, having successfully avoided the cell-like metal lift, thick with cigarette smoke. All the swimmers and their parents were to stay together in these rented university halls in Sheffield that year. Roan wanted the parents supporting the team's efforts, helping to cook meals, on a roster of driving and washing up, so the swimmers could have more down time between races. Amelia and I were sharing a room; we had been bonded together again by the events of the last couple of months: the end of junior school, the summer of being sixteen – no longer the babies – Julia's situation, and how dark the boarding house had become. My mum was over, and she was sharing a room with Amelia's mum. They got stuck in, and for the days before the competition, all the parents rubbed along awkwardly and politely as we went off to train at Ponds Forge and came back to fill the floor of our halls with chlorine and wet towels.

'I would rather not PB for three years than be one of them.' It was one of the older boys from Cardiff Swimming Club. I recognised his voice because he was friends with Dan and Jenkins. At first, I wondered why he wasn't with them in Helsinki at the European Juniors, and then I remembered he must be on the Welsh team for the Commonwealths later that year; a lot of the swimmers were preparing to train hard through the competitions of the summer so they could peak in Delhi in the autumn. I made these mental calculations as I pulled damp socks onto wet feet, balancing on one leg at a time, my toes perched on the edge of my trainers. The competition started the next day and we'd just done our final training session. A girl's voice came over the top of the changing room next: 'Easy for you to say, you swam three personal bests at trials, some of us haven't for at least a season.' – 'Yeah, but have you seen the way they walk around like fucking robots?' It was the boy again.

'They're like fucking drones, and Roan is their master.' There was some laughter. 'It's like a hive mind,' another boy piped up and the girl laughed along with them. 'You don't know what a hive mind is,' the boy turned on her. I felt her embarrassment as my own, but they weren't done yet. 'Do you remember when that Chay girl went out after trials, you guys weren't there, you know, the Black girl who won the breaststroke, yeah . . .' He paused and I listened closer. 'So, everyone went out on the last night of trials, and she got into the club and then one of their coaches was there and she literally got army-marched out by this fat coach holding her by the arm!' They all laughed. 'If you have even an ounce of talent at Plymouth, you're screwed!' the girl proclaimed. I was currently ranked third in the world. I was screwed. We were his trophies, and I was the shiniest of them all, paraded around poolside but just a body. Because in my mind, his hand was on my neck all the time and with his face inches from mine. He took my love for the sport and he crushed it with one large hand, while with the other pushed me forward to the blocks over and over. This was how it felt. I came out of the changing room and walked past them, deliberately but without looking. They all fell into silence. I was a giant on poolside now, British Champion gracing Youth Nationals with my presence before jetting off for my senior British debut. Or so it appeared. But I had never been smaller.

Little did Roan know, bringing everyone together like this was going to do more to his club than he'd bargained for. Our world of open secrets was about to bleed outside its formerly well-guarded walls. One of the younger boys on the squad –

from the Home Counties, mild-mannered but keenly observing – had obviously been telling his mum some of what was going on. She'd never had any contact with the other parents and the stories had seemed far-fetched and not worth verifying until now, where the hurdle for conversation was low. She started talking while chopping vegetables one evening with some of the other parents. That's what Amelia's mum told mine. And slowly, small fragments of this world were pieced together over dinner preparation. By day two, some of the parents had spoken to their kids. Some of the boys' parents were horrified. Mothers walked around the halls with hair pulled back severely from mascara-less faces red from recent crying. It started to feel like a funeral. Some of the parents didn't care, but only a few. By the end of the third day, Roan had found out and a meeting had been called. My mother, always a fearless crusader in the face of crisis, started shaking the trees. She started with me. I was one of the few girls who had never been on the boys' floor, which had always made me feel left out but now it was going to protect me. The same boy who had originally told his mum had also told her that Ella – the girl from the minibus – and I weren't involved. My mum and I sat in the car outside and the first drop of summer rain hit the windscreen as she interrogated me, insistent: 'What did you do?' she asked over and over. 'Nothing,' I pleaded, 'I didn't do anything, I didn't do anything wrong.'

The rumours were that some of the boys passed some of the girls around. At the boarding house it was bad, but at competitions it was way worse. It was also normal, or it had come to feel that way. In my mind, it had all started when talk of sex first entered the common room, which now felt like a lifetime ago. We were inured to it all. Someone's body was too big, some girl had a 'fat arse'. The boys talked about our cunts and called us cunts in front of everyone on poolside, and in the minibus as we drove back and forth from Roan's poolside to the prison we called home. We used to joke that our laundry numbers were our prison numbers. Prisoner number 202, that was me, the tiny labels ironed into all my clothes that made me comply. It seemed funny to us that our parents were surprised. 'They sent us off to prison,' Amelia said to me, 'what did they expect?' Between the heats and the finals of the fourth day, Amelia's mum found me in our room alone. I had stayed at their house a couple of times, I knew her husband and Amelia's brother. She sat down opposite me, and my breathing became fast and heavy, all through my nose and high up in my chest, as she asked me the same questions my mother had. I told her Amelia had done nothing wrong and I told her I didn't know about any of the rumours, and that I couldn't confirm anything she'd heard.

In the days that followed, the allegations kept coming. My mum got in touch with the head of boarding at the school to ask them if I could live in the school boarding house instead of the swimming one so I could stay at Plymouth. That was a dead end. It felt like the rumours couldn't be quashed quickly enough. My mum asked to speak to the headmaster, but she couldn't get a meeting. Amelia's mum and mine explored the possibility of us living in a house together near school so we could finish sixth form and carry on swimming. After all this activity my mum wasn't particularly welcome at the emergency team meeting. It had been suggested that she was riling the other parents up and distracting everyone from the important task at hand: finishing the season off on a high, with a great Nationals. In the meeting, Roan gave a rousing speech about how much everyone had sacrificed, leaned on the money everyone had ploughed into their children, his programme and, ultimately, everyone's success. But reality had punctured our bubble, and the one our parents had been living in too. And reality was startling. I had been a perfect item and protected from this reality so that I could remain that way. But now, a small crack had appeared in my underside; this week had split open a little hole inside me just big enough for the first raindrop of a thunderstorm to make its way in, or the first bit of evil to crawl out of Pandora's box. The real world got in, slowly at first but soon it would come faster and faster, like a metasta-sising disease. And my world, the one that made me the perfect athlete, disappeared. The truth was, I had felt safer inside that bubble, with all the pain and all the rules. We liked to do what we were told – after all, we were children.

XX

Sometimes the discomfort is in your mind, sometimes it's not. But discomfort was something I had been taught to endure, and after learning to endure it, I learned to respect it, and through respect I'd found a love for it too. I returned to my rituals to block out the noise of the last week in Sheffield. I let my conscious mind focus on the granular tasks of swimming: breathe, stroke count, the phases of my leg kick. They coached us to focus on these small components in training so that our subconscious minds could deliver the thing we'd spent years preparing for: the race. Behind the block I would keep my clothes on until just before the first whistle. There are two. Then, after they announced the names of the swimmers, I would kneel down by the water's edge with one hand on the lip of the pool around the touchpad and splash myself with water, gathering it to me, trying to take it out of the pool, making it mine with as much noise as I could. I would splash water into my mouth and then blow it out hard. Take a freeze frame of any race and at the centre of it you'll see the winner looking up while everyone else is locked into their starting position. I don't know how I learned to do this, but one day I just started, and it stuck. The sharp whistle first, two blasts: get ready. Then the longer one, staccato at the end: get on the block. When the silence fell and everyone bent down to curl their fingers around the front of their board, I'd remain upright as they crouched, and then with my hands still wet I'd clap. Twice. So loudly it echoed around the stands and then I'd let out a sharp exhale. I'd make the start marshal wait for me, and my competitors too, just for a split second; I'd make everyone in the stadium wait for me, then I'd bend down. Over the years, the more confident I had become the longer I would make them wait. And although I didn't feel it, I used this at Nationals to get through my finals.

Despite what had happened in the halls, I'd had to find a way to let the drama fade into the background. Because in the foreground there was also physical pain. The large piriformis muscle connecting my tailbone to the top of my leg and across my pelvis had become inflamed. It was compressing my sciatic nerve, and the inflammation had caused a numbness down the right side of my buttock and into the back of my hamstring. The piriformis muscle aids in almost every movement and the sciatic nerve is the longest and largest in your body. I couldn't sit and I could barely walk. Julia lowered me onto a dense rubber orb the size of a tennis ball. I felt the nerve light up and send a signal to my brain that made my eyelid twitch so hard it felt like one side of my face was drooping. Overexercising and repetitive motion. It was a classic breaststroke condition. I was lucky; hypermobile, with strong joints and even stronger quads and shoulders, I never got injured, but I could now feel my body starting to fray. Before I got in the pool for warm-up, I would swing my arms, crossing them in front of and then above my head and then again behind, so violently it looked like I might shake them loose from their sockets. Then I would repeat this with my legs, swinging them back and forth, one at a time, holding onto a rail with one hand, or the shoulder of a teammate. We would move down our body, checking every muscle with specific movements. Rotate the neck left and right, then forward and back, fingers to the floor, bent forward with our forehead on our knees, hips rotated, and then hip flexors pulled out on the floor in a low lunge, and we'd carry on, all the way down to our ankles. That week, before my second race in Sheffield, the muscle in my buttock was so engorged that every time I moved, I was a freshly branded cow, a red-hot poker burn sending a searing pain shooting up my back and down my leg at the same time. I competed through it.

I won the semi-final of the 100-metre breaststroke in 1.09.97. It was slow and it scared me, but I told myself and anyone else who would listen that it was only the semi-final, and I would be on a flight to Budapest before they swam the final race. In the months after trials, with new analysis from America, Roan had instructed Julia to try to change my stroke so I could get higher and angulate more on the surface of the water. The 100-metre breaststroke had become my nemesis, and I already felt like it was beyond me but now, going into Europeans, I felt like I didn't even know how to swim anymore. For the first time, I felt superstitious. The warm-up, which was just meant to heat your muscles and awaken your nervous system, also started to whisper to me, 'That catch wasn't very good – maybe your feel for the water is gone. That dive was shaky and slow – do you think your taper was wrong?' It spoke softly as I climbed out at the 15-metre mark and looked at Julia's face, screwed up at her stopwatch, looking at the time I'd just swum. 'What if it's just you, you've finally lost the magic? It was probably going to happen at some point. Did you really think you were going to have it forever and you'd just carry on getting better and better?' it continued in a conspiratorial tone.

Until the British Championships and the scrutiny and the press that followed, even though it had always been fraught and controlling my nerves had been a long-fought battle, I had always believed that I would be able to find another gear. That my edge was unlosable. But now I felt cursed. Perversely, when I swam any other stroke, or any other distance, I still held the promise and the raw power that had first got me here. Although not a freestyle sprinter, I had come second in the 50 metres at the Nationals that year; 26.49, a decent time, 0.1 of a second off gold. I could still race, fast, just not in the one stroke people wanted me to.

In Budapest, I was about to make history by putting on that cap, royal blue with the Union Jack and 'GBR' in bold white writing. With that swimming cap on and my Black body poised on the block, I would become the first. And even though I was ranked second into the 100-metre and first into the 50-metre breaststroke events going into the European Championships, I was still an outsider on the British team, because I was the youngest, because I was new and because I was different. The fallout from Sheffield hung in the air between me and Roan and we had to take that all the way to Budapest; because of me, he was now on the British coaching team. He knew I was leaving him; my mum had made that abundantly clear before she left Sheffield the week before, so now all that was left in our relationship was pure transaction and, beneath that, my sense of loss. But more than anything I was truly terrified of him, and with neither Julia nor my mother here to protect me, the fear felt more real than it ever had.

On the way into the stadium, a light crowd gathered each day with printed picture cards of the swimmers. It was hot, the pool was outside, and we wore sleeveless white pullovers with hoods and mesh panels of red and blue. Most of the senior swimmers were from Loughborough, Nottingham and Bath, and they'd all known each other for almost a whole Olympic cycle. They laughed confidently at the entrance and signed pictures of themselves without breaking conversation with each other. I held my two hands behind my back because I didn't know what else to do with them and went onto poolside to warm up. *The Telegraph* wrote the big debut article – I was 'a complete one-off' – it was positive, almost glowing. Roan was only mentioned once, a small footnote in relation to me. 'Ajulu-Bushell to Become First Black Woman to Swim for Britain', the headline read. Roan wouldn't talk about it; he barely looked at me, and, oddly, apart from all the people who watched me on poolside because I was the only one who looked like me, no one else really looked *at* me either.

I told you about the perfect race. There were so many imperfect races, but this one was the worst. Two sharp, clipped trills. I step forward. Sun in my eyes and a tightness in my knuckles as I visualise my dive. I step up. My legs shake on the blocks as I slam my right foot into the adjustable wedge at the back and it jams, almost pushing me forward and into the pool. *Breathe. Calm down*, I tell myself. Weight forward as I try to find the moment of counterbalance, but my legs don't react. I try to tense them: nothing. The light from the pool reflects off my googles and back into my eyes. Never turn your head to the start marshal. I do, and his watch bounces light off the water and straight into my retina. Panic. As I start to empty the thoughts from my mind, I find one that won't leave. 'You can't', it says. I try to forget, but all the negative thoughts are with me, surrounding me as I crouch on the block. *Come on, come on.* I think I can hear the button click, but I'm too late. The buzzer sounds. Move. My mind responds and pulls my body forward. I land sloppy, in the choppy water I've made for myself. The angle is too small; I'm not deep enough.

I force myself deeper underwater and lose my count straight away. One, two, I'm rising too fast, can't wait for three. Pull. A camera on a train track underwater punctuates the silence with a click as it hits a join on its track and my head moves, imperceptibly, but once again I'm drawn from streamline and out of focus. This is desperate. *Get up, get above the surface, you're wasting time.* The water is treacle. With superhuman effort, I move my arms to change my direction of travel. I don't know where my hips are. My body is so tired but it's all I can do to rush to the shallows. I kick from the bottom of my stomach to my ankles, there's no tension in my feet and my ankles knock into each other, I know they aren't aligned. Two more mistakes. I'm only 5 centimetres below the surface now and I start to let my lungs guide me up. I try for soft feet, soft hands, tight body, hard mind, but everything's soft. My body is moving in the dark, disorganised but hopeful. My hands try to find the catch, but I slip through the water and watch my little finger disappear from my peripheral vision. They should never be out of view. I hear Roan's voice in my head: hope is not a strategy. *What's the stroke count?* I ask myself. *I don't know.* Yes, you do. Panic again. *I think it's eight.*

The stroke count is wrong. Twenty-five metres finally arrives and I get there like a home video stuck on one frame, juddering in slow motion. Lactic acid greets me as well but the wall is a mirage, never moving closer. Paint thinner burns through my lungs and the bile rises in my mouth like I've just taken a shot of bleach. My head's under the flags and I already know I'm short on the wall. I watch others turn. I try to move quickly but my body has never felt bigger. I can't speed up. Trapped in a world of half speed, I watch my hands as my brain tells them to retract. They don't move. With every moment I spend here I lose energy to the wall; I don't have any to spare. The lactic acid has taken over my brain now. Filling up my eyelids, the world is fuzzy. The yellow touchpad, my red fingernails and the black line down its centre that meets the tiles on the pool's floor; through blurred vision I see these three colours blend to form a Mondrian tile against the wall. And I see my nail varnish, painted proudly a few days earlier – in anticipation of podium photographs – to match my new kit. Pain unimaginable and getting stronger. *Breathe.* I can't. I turn. *Finally.* And as I push off the wall, I realise I'm going to come last.

I want to stop. I have to, but there's 35 metres to go. My head lolls back and forth with every out-of-time stroke, like a ragdoll who's never known rhythm. Slowly, everything begins to melt into the background. The lactic acid has devoured my pride and my brain is shutting down, spreading darkness from the base of my neck, coating my body in despair. I'm drowning. My face is contorted, I think I'm crying now. The sorrow is total. All the things I've concealed from myself appear like phantoms in the water, floating around my legs and pulling me under. They stay to haunt me. I can just about hear the dull, faraway sound of cheers. But all I can register is pain. Without warning, it's over. I lift my head out of the water, but I don't look upward at the scoreboard. My nose touches the water's surface like I want to inhale it and sink below. I wonder how I will climb out now that my body doesn't work anymore. And my very last thought, before my disintegrating mind shuts down totally to protect me from the shock of this memory, is *I never want to do this again.*

I speak to no one and make straight for the swim-down pool. After a race, the first thing you do is go to see your coach. That was the last thing I was going to do. The Russian girl swam sub-1.09 and her heat, the final heat, put me twenty-fourth, eight places away from progressing to the semi-final. I was out. I had imagined the tears through the race, but they came quickly now as I let the sun beat down on my back and the gravity of the deep swim-down pool pull my body into a deeper position on the water's surface. I swam freestyle without breathing so I couldn't see who was around me or who was coming and carried on until I heard my name. I stopped at the end and curled my hand around the lip of the wall, and he stepped closer, so close his foot was inches from my fingers. 'I don't know what happened . . .' I started to say. 'I can tell you what happened: you didn't prepare properly, did you . . .' he started. I looked down. He wasn't asking. 'I've already told the Director that you're a lazy athlete so don't bother coming up with anything else.' His voice was raised now. 'You're not committed. You know, this isn't my fault, is it? You're the one who went out there and humiliated yourself.' He paused to breathe. I was shaking in the pool below him. He looked down at me, his frame blocking the sun so I could see the look in his eyes, his tongue coming slowly out of the right-hand corner of his mouth, darting and wet as he moistened his lips to speak; 'I'm done with you.'

When I woke, I immediately knew something was wrong. Outside my hotel room it was quiet. It was past 9.30 a.m., we'd had an early flight home. I'd missed it. My body was in shut-down mode and I was still in shock from what had happened in the race and the swim-down pool, but it didn't stop my cortisol spiking as I went into panic once more. I didn't bother trying to use the hotel phone; I would explain my phone bill to my mum later. I dialled. Nothing. By the time I got through to her, I was hyperventilating. Between gasps I managed to say, 'I'm still in Budapest.' – 'Achi, what do you mean?' – 'I mean I missed my flight and I'm still in Budapest.' I was crying now. 'You're at the airport?' she demanded. 'No,' I sniffed, 'I'm still at the hotel.'

XXI

In Doha the news felt far away, but in the weeks beforehand it had still managed to get inside me. 'Ajulu-Bushell Out to Make Amends for European Horror', the *Guardian* headline read on the first Sunday in October. I'd trained myself to avoid the coverage at all costs, but somehow small pockets of it still found their way to me and this one I could have done without. 'Some have been predictably quick to claim that Ajulu-Bushell is living refutation of the ugly old assertion that Black Africans cannot swim at the top level,' it stated. I bet he'd felt clever writing that. The article went on to talk about my 'terrible competition' in Budapest and how the Commonwealth Games would be my 'first chance to make amends'. That same week, I saw the comment on the SwimSwam website. An article about who was going to be head coach of British Swimming after the man Roan had been talking to in Rome retired: 'I was hoping for Roan,' the nameless man wrote. 'He did some amazing things at Plymouth.' Then he reeled off a list of names. I went to the place inside me where joy had been banished when I read the last line: 'He coached Achieng Ajulu-Bushell back when she used to be good.' It was really important that I found a way to block this out over the training camp. The week in Doha was significant, and the Commonwealth Games was a big stage. I didn't have to make amends, I reminded myself. You don't owe them an apology with your body, these people who believe the most I can be is an anomaly. The thing that I couldn't get out of my mind, that was starting to make wider the crack that had first appeared that week in Sheffield, was the way so many of these articles ended with the same prediction, and this one was no different: 'The girl, you would guess, is going places. And not just in the pool.' My education was tugging harder and harder at the fabric of my life, and in the downtime in Doha, between training sessions as I sat trying to make sense of my politics homework – already mounting from two weeks of missed school – I wondered at what point my life in the pool would ruin the one I could have outside it.

Less than a month after Budapest, my mum had found me a new school, a new club and a new place to live; and just as Roan was done with me, she was completely done with him. I moved to London in September 2010, after narrowly avoiding being sent to Bath. I don't know how she did it, but I was back in a new pool before my first day of sixth form. At my new school, I was desperate not to be the swimmer. I wore ripped jeans and army boots with an oversized jumper, chunky silver rings. Over the summer, in the short week between the end of the last swimming season and the start of this one, I'd visited my family back in Kenya and got a weave. My hair was still relaxed and made artificially longer by the tracks of extensions that had been sewn into three cornrows. My face was puffy and tired, pale in contrast to the dark eyeliner I wore almost permanently and my over-drawn eyebrows. I was a new version of me, one that wanted two different lives simultaneously.

In the first few weeks I watched incredulous as girls as young as twelve got on the red double-deckers outside Ealing station, deep in conversation, seemingly without checking the number on the front or where they were swiping their Oyster cards. I navigated the short journey from my godparents' house to school with their daughter, who was three years my junior and had the same nonchalant confidence about her. After school I would also take the bus to training, and out the window I started to see the narrowness of the identity swimming had offered up to me. 'Are you that girl from the BBC?' one of the bus drivers asked me one day as a queue of girls stood behind me. 'I don't think so,' I replied. I didn't want my cover blown so soon. I made new friends quickly, and just as quickly I settled into a newfound freedom, navigating my life with fewer controls around my time. How much people were giving up to make this work had no bearing on what I was feeling; and how much I wanted to push against swimming's natural constraints on my life seemingly had no bearing on them, either. At least twice a week, my godmother would drive me to morning training at 5 a.m. For the other morning sessions, my coach would pick me up. London was hard: pool time was expensive, and so we moved around a lot. On Mondays we had to abandon the Ealing pool and drive out past Ruislip to a 33-metre pool in Highgrove. But London was also diverse. And what little of it I saw in those first few weeks planted small seeds of intrigue in the same crack that I was watering with thoughts of university and International Relations degrees.

My body had changed dramatically and almost overnight. I was less than six months from seventeen; between my mounting hormones and the slight decrease in intensity of my training since I left Plymouth, I was gaining weight. Not enough for anyone else to say anything to me, but after three years of fat-testing, it was more than enough for me to start saying things to myself. I felt big all the time, and now my over-developed shoulders had boobs and bum to match. It started slowly. After morning training I'd have at least two croissants in addition to my breakfast of fruit and porridge and the Nutri-Grain bar I'd have on the way there. I was also starving from dinner the night before; no longer eating from a canteen buffet meant I never quite had enough food, and this would kick me quickly into overeating the next day. I spent a considerable amount of time pulling at my stomach as I felt my costumes get incrementally tighter and I held onto the folds around my armpit. I knew the coach at my new club was going to weigh me soon; it would be nothing like as public as at Plymouth, but I was embarrassed, nonetheless. I felt I had so much to prove, the hotshot who'd just come up from the best club in the country and also crashed out very publicly at the Europeans. 'And she's fat now.' I started throwing up after dinner.

The week before I was due to leave for a ten-day training camp in Doha before flying on to Delhi with Team England, we had a late-night visitor. My godmother summoned me downstairs at 11 p.m. on a Wednesday evening, which meant I had to be up for morning training in less than six hours. There were three of them; my mum had told my godparents this might happen, and British Swimming never stopped sending me emails about WADA, the World Anti-Doping Agency. I had been drug-tested before, but I'd never believed, even after filling out my whereabouts to specify an hour slot every day when they could come and make me pee in a cup, that they would ever turn up. Plain-clothed, with official badges that they kept in their pockets and flashed at my godmother as they came in and didn't bother showing to me. I had never not had a chaperone and even though I acted blasé, like it happened all the time, I had only ever done this once. The woman and her male colleague walked me upstairs to the bathroom. My godmother was by the bathroom door, the door stayed open, and the male agent waited outside while his female colleague came into the bathroom I used every day, the same one I often threw up in, patted me down and made me tuck my T-shirt into my bra so it stayed hiked up while I peed in the special glass jar she'd given me as she watched. I had never felt strange about any facet of my swimming world until now. I felt something akin to shame as my godmother witnessed them make me screw the lid onto my own special jar of urine and label and box it up myself, so that I was sure it hadn't been tampered with. My two lives were not easy to navigate between, and the more effort I made to keep one from the other, the more shame I felt when they collided.

*

I had to wear a tiny bib with my name on and ascend a small, makeshift stage in a conference room in our brand-new hotel in Doha for the ill-conceived initiation. The team was mostly in their early twenties, and even though I was still sixteen, I'd shed a lot of naivety since the summer. Team England was broader and less bullish than the senior British Swimming team, and the Commonwealth Games was closest to the feeling of an Olympics, with a proper Athletes' Village with every kind of athlete present and teams made up of smaller teams of every sport. I was passing time on the training camp and tolerating my subjection to the older swimmers' rituals because I knew that when we left Qatar for India and settled in the purpose-built Athletes' Village in Dehli, I would get to see beyond the insular world of the pool. Half of the world's 2008 Olympic teams would be there, and I would also get to see my family. When we arrived in Delhi we found the team accommodation was in tower blocks, still largely empty, with bathroom tiles for flooring. We were given our own duvets, printed with the Games' colours: 'Delhi 2010' they said, in purple writing on stiff orange cotton. The whole village was half built. Exposed pipes jutted up everywhere through the red earth, and the bus to the pool was fifty minutes each way. Everyone else got ill almost immediately, but to me, it felt a lot like being back in Kenya – something like home.

The lanyard and its laminated tag hung slightly off-centre around my neck as I sat on the bus with my headphones on watching Delhi as we snaked across highways in dappled sunlight. The music in my ears had been my old pump-up song. I remembered the girl that was me with the hard face and the strong back and clenched jaw. Fierce and preparing. I hoped if I listened to her music, I might reclaim some of her power too. You've got to swim it out, swim what you feel. Leave it all in the pool. That advice had come from the team's sport psychologist earlier today. We were heading to the pool for the semi-final of the Women's 50-metre breaststroke, and I was in lane three, right next to Leisel Jones. I couldn't swim what I felt because I felt paralysed. And my parents' presence only served to compound that; of all the times they could have come it had to be now, at what I was starting to believe was the end of all things. I didn't want them to show up anymore, at least not here and now; there was a time when I had, and they couldn't be there.

When it was over, I watched the race back repeatedly on the BBC website. We were in the first of two semi-finals, eight swimmers in each. Strong dive, something of who I was at the very beginning. I stared into the screen and tried to work out if it was the angle, a trick mirror, or if I had really been ahead all the way to 25 metres. I watched it again and looked for the exact moment I'd started to spin, around 37 metres. I could hear Julia's voice in my head: 'Stroke rate's a bit too high isn't it, my love,' then she'd clap me on the cheeks, and we'd prepare for the final together. I was so lonely. I missed the hold of Plymouth, having somebody to watch this race with, someone who knew the exact timing of my pull-out to tell me if I'd rushed it even a fraction. I watched the race again. Head-to-head with Leisel Jones, double Olympic champion. I had watched her on TV – as I was watching us both now – at the Olympics in 2004 when I was eight years old. I recognised something of the girl in lane three now, and that was almost more painful than the stranger I'd been to myself at the Europeans. I was still there; in moments of this race, I could see flashes of brilliance. And as the race came to an end again on the small screen in front of me, I watched our names flash up on the water, 1. Jones, 2. Ajulu-Bushell. I wanted to turn to someone and say, 'Look, look at this, I've waited a lifetime for this moment, ever since watching the Athens Olympics on a TV in Kenya over six years ago. And now that's my name, I'm here, I made it!' Only there was no one there, and I was buried under a year of shame; in this reality, I hadn't made it and I wasn't going to. In the final I came fifth, and then I got drug-tested again straight afterwards; it took so long that I had to take the late bus home and I didn't get to see my parents again. The only thing worse, I decided, would have been coming fourth.

Recover

XXII

'Do not remember me
as disaster
nor as the keeper of secrets
I am a fellow rider in the cattle cars . . .
saying we cannot waste time
only ourselves.'

Audre Lorde

I grabbed the twenty-pound note from out of the boy's hand
and Lara grabbed my arm and we ran shrieking through the
field of tents back in the direction of the main stage, near the
silent disco, where our camp was pitched in a circle. The sun
hadn't come out once, but I'd never felt warmer. Absinthe and
laughter and music that moved between my ears and down
into my chest. I watched my best friend have her first kiss
pushed up against the rails at the front of a side stage. Behind

me, a grid of sodium light burst on at the bridge of the song; if I could have stayed there watching her forever, I would have, the yellow glow illuminating her smiling face over the boy's shoulder and her hands in his tousled hair as she looked for me every so often. I stood alone, beaming back at her, and listened to everyone screaming the lyrics around me. The words hit the stage and came back at us from the speakers. I was drunk and ecstatic. She was safe. I didn't know the boy but her long dark hair kept her in my sight as the crowd weaved around us and the song played on. I'd known I was being half bribed when I got dropped off at the train station the day before by my parents with my half-ticket for the last two nights of the festival. And one of our group had come to meet me at the entrance with the wrist band of someone who had already left. I hadn't seen my London friends since the end of our exams and now it was late August. My red lipstick had stained the corners of my mouth over the first twenty-four hours and my stepdad's blue T-shirt with thin white stripes down it was tied at my waist, the borrowed wellies that I'd have to clean and give back on Monday pinching my flat feet at the bridge. I put both my hands in the air, tipped my chin up and joined in as the crowd all sang at once. At the end of the weekend, I knew I was going to be forced back into the water and the freedoms of my life in London would be behind me. Only a year up ahead now, this time next summer, the threat of the Olympics loomed.

A disposable camera caught me sideways on a camping chair with bright pink writing on my arm. I knew from the angle that I would hate the way it looked in the picture, my shoulder protruding out and forward and my arm so dense with muscle it looked fat when not tensed. My body was fighting and losing a battle with biology; as I marched towards eighteen my hormones raged, my boobs grew almost daily and a waist I'd never had became visible above my hips, which were still narrow but now coated in fat. There is a myth that beauty is acceptance, but I didn't know a self-love that didn't adhere to some type of aesthetic standard. I felt so much bigger than I was. A woman's body pasted on top of an athlete's.

Those days in the festival fields were a farewell and also an introduction. To a life I had never had and didn't even know that I might have wanted. I had had glimpses, but this experience came with the freedom of being completely untethered, in a field for two days with my seventeen-year-old friends with no parents or coaches, no home time, no bedtime, no up at 4.30 a.m. for training. Only a handful of times over the last five years had I ever really been jealous of the normal kids doing normal things on normal weekends. I didn't know enough about what they did to miss it, and also I hadn't cared because I was exceptional, and I understood the nature of my exceptionalness as being part of my outsider status. I'd even liked it. Being different, I'd believed, was only a half-curse, and a long time ago, almost subconsciously, I had decided to delight in the separation it created between me and my peers. A complex debate of nature versus nurture had been playing out since I was just old enough to walk, one in which I didn't know if I had become the way I was because I was different or because being different had made me the way I was. Maybe winning had been a salve, my salvation, a way to block it all out, an answer to questions I didn't even have the words to ask. But as that weekend revealed how much life other people were living, I saw those questions in the eyes of everyone around me. Questions about my big lips and dark eyes against my brown, European-looking face, 'a lightie', with some privilege that dark-skinned Black women don't possess. A horrible kind of power, a different kind of fetishisation – a 'not you, but them' kind of distinction. I saw boys and I knew they liked me, and I hated the fact that I believed they would have liked me more if my hair were softer, longer, and if I'd looked more like my two younger sisters, who are both white and both quintessentially beautiful; and I hated the fact that we shared physical features, so in my darkest moments I felt robbed – robbed of my whiteness. I didn't know how else to feel. Only that my Blackness was a hindrance to my white beauty, that it prevented boys from liking me the way that I believed they should, but more than that, it stopped me from moving through the world in an undisturbed silence. I didn't know my brown skin could make my life richer – it had only ever made it more complicated.

Things had unravelled in my mind over the months since the Commonwealth Games. I'd placed fifth and eighth; it was defensible, but it was also my last roll of the dice. I didn't know it, but I also did know it: I was done. If I had swum even close to my best, I would have made the podium, and without that affirmation I could sense inside my chest a kind of heartbreak

– that I didn't think I'd ever let myself fully acknowledge – taking over. In January, I'd failed all my mock exams. I'd scoffed when my head of sixth form told me how far behind I'd fallen after I got back from Delhi at the end of the previous year, then there were Ds and Es arriving in comically big red letters to prove it. I'd hidden the evidence from my new friends; it wasn't the kind of school where people failed any exams. I'd tried to hide it from my mum too, and my godparents, and for a time I was successful. Sneaky and secretive, always lying to someone at any given moment and miserable. I used the fact that my swimming-schooling-living-world in London wasn't joined up, unlike my time in Plymouth. In the moments that I went between these places, no one was in charge. It's not that people didn't care where I was or what I was doing, it was just that I was out of Roan's panopticon, and I exploited the parts of my life that were out of view. On Wednesdays when we had PE – me exempt because of my swimming – I was given the time back to catch up on work; instead, I used to get on the bus from school to travel to the part of Notting Hill that's overlooked by Westway and hang out with a boy in a tower block. I did his economics homework, sat suggestively on the single bed in his small bedroom. In the same skipping-PE era, I lay on my stomach with a fuchsia-pink bra on, home alone at another house and crossed my ankles, facing the soles of my feet to someone else's boyfriend. 'Put your legs down, it's not *Sex and the City*,' he said to me. The line shot straight to my core. I was watching myself in that moment – like all self-obsessed teenage girls, the soundtrack of my late youth was my own internal monologue – but my performance was naive. Immediately deconstructed, it was clear to me that I didn't know how to be in this dry and complicated world outside the pool. I decided then that I would have to learn. Some weekends I would go to Lara's for a sleepover, and we'd go out on a Saturday night to Portobello Road. There I learned how to get into bars without an ID, how to identify the person who will buy you a drink but not ask for anything more. We'd take hundreds of pictures, documenting the simple joy of being out, free, in the dark of the night with no supervision, high on the fact that whatever we were doing was known only to us.

After another set of bad mock results, there was an intervention from my mother, 'You can't carry on like this.' It was overdramatic, I thought. I had spent three months doing just a quarter of what it seemed everyone else my age had done for the past three years. 'It's not fair,' I retorted. As soon as I said it, I heard how stupid it sounded – of course it wasn't fair. My godparents had agreed to be my guardians when I'd moved up to London after that last summer at Plymouth, and my parents paid them something every month. My mum paid my private school fees herself, and always had. I'd always had scholarships, but they never awarded more than 50 per cent. My sisters were growing up without me and I already felt grown up, which I'd done without them. How much time had my mum had to spend on my behalf? And how much had all the travel cost, the petrol, the plane tickets? 'I just don't want to do it anymore,' I said at last. I heard my mum sigh into the phone, long and low. 'It's too much,' I followed up softly. 'Why don't we just get you through your exams and then we can reassess?' she said. It felt cold, in her voice and in my room and in my bones. Certainly, I'd pushed people away, but I didn't want them to stop trying to reach me.

We struck a deal. I would train only three times a week for the next month. It was radical, insane even, to my coach and the other swimmers, that I would dial down my training a year before the Olympics for the sake of my education. These were the exams that would get me into university, and subconsciously I think I hoped this would get me out of the pool altogether. But in the background a plan was already being put in place to get me back in the pool. My family were getting ready to leave Kenya and move back to the UK, they'd settled on Oxford; so, after only a year in London, against my will I thought, I would be leaving too. Julia had left Plymouth, and Roan was now the head coach of a club in Oxford. My silence was large and loud, and everyone had taken to asking what was wrong. 'I'm fine,' I always replied. 'Are you sure you're okay?' came the follow-up. 'I'm fine,' I'd repeat. I couldn't say anything else. 'Whatever happened to you in Plymouth, in Hungary, with Roan, you know, it's not your fault,' they'd say. I was so defeated, so beaten, that all I could offer were monosyllabic replies.

In the two school terms since I'd returned from the Commonwealth Games, I'd been introduced to a version of myself I'd never met. Not a new kind of me, but someone different altogether. I saw other spaces in the world that I could work into and thought eventually they might be shaped like me. I stayed up and out late. I hung out with people I didn't know and threw up drunk in their bathrooms. The rule-fol-lowing-adult-pleaser was ebbing away, still clutching at control with a guilt that gnawed at me daily, but there was someone new battling for power too. She was smart and angry. Angry that the world was so big and, even though she'd seen so much of it, she'd never noticed. On the train back from that festival, picking methodically at the dried mud splatters that had caked up the backs of my legs, I looked out at the fuzzy green beyond the window. Oxford had been grey when I'd first arrived. We'd spent two weeks house-hunting and staying with my parents' friends. I remembered one of the first nights, on a sofa in the front room of a house I didn't know, there was a low hum: not the vibration of traffic from a West London road punctuated by sirens, but a hum that came from within. I woke my mum. 'What is that?' I asked earnestly. She came out of her room slowly and we walked towards the stairs which creaked, and the humming felt closer. Mum padded around the front room, listening carefully with an exaggerated cocked ear and her socks muffling the light sound of her toes. She came to a stop outside the door under the stairs and beckoned me. As I approached, the hum rose to a crescendo. She put her hand on the knob and twisted. It wasn't locked. As she opened it, a swarm of bluebottle flies exploded into the room. I screamed and looked at my mum wide-eyed. She'd just left Kenya; nearly eighteen years she'd done in Africa, through post-election violence, shoot-ings, carjacking, safari mishaps and roads cut into cliffs. She looked at me, more bewildered than I'd ever seen her. 'I don't know what we're doing here,' she said, and she said it so quietly it was almost mouthed. We stood together in the room of flies, both beyond the unknown, and somehow it made me feel better.

A phrase I'd never been able to shake returned to me in this new city. 'She speaks with a cut-glass British accent,' a journalist had written in a piece from an interview just after I became British Champion. As opposed to what? How else should I speak? I'd never been able to say out loud what I thought he really meant, not even to myself. I'd been ashamed to make it about class and betray my mother; but now I was ready for a proper translation: 'She speaks surprisingly well actually, knows lots of words, no African accent at all.' My father would have found that funny, but I still couldn't. In London I had shed the Plymouth twang that I'd adopted to help me try and fit in and had settled into a flatter, more natural southern English lilt. I sounded more like my stepdad and the way his family spoke, well-schooled, they said. We found a place to live in Oxford, and my now very real cut-glass British accent echoed through it – this city, and all the cream-coloured furniture in our new red-brick terraced house by the river. I hated it here, but I could never go back. I could see that so clearly. A new cultural world was opening up in front of me, like a doorway I was being forced to walk through. I'd developed my own taste somewhere in the past year: somehow, I'd found the time to like fresh coffee and vintage clothing. The trauma of so much of my training had kept me so feral; it was even foreign to think. But now I studied politics, and only my irreverence to my new private girls' school kept me distanced from the conservative overtones in my class. And the white Mini Coopers and eighteenth birthdays in white marquee tents were so affronting to the memory of my reality – my old reality at Plymouth and my childhood in Kenya and South Africa – that even when I got invited to their parties, or sat in the back seat of their cars, they didn't seem real. I couldn't go back, even if I wanted to. I could feel the veneer of middle-class suburbia settling over me, customs I hadn't known existed and unspoken rules within gradations of wealth that competed for oxygen and skiing holidays. And I was back in the pool. 4.30 a.m. remembered me well. Maybe winning hadn't been my salvation. Maybe it had just been a state of existence, a predetermined destiny I had always had within me that had oozed out like just-opened toothpaste, flowing forth with no pressure applied. Now, I was a rolled-up tube, trying to get at the very last bit. There wasn't much, and I was sick of squeezing.

XXIII

'I hope you're doing okay?' Paul started as I sat down. 'Mum and I had a little chat the other day about you and your swimming and I've been thinking about it a lot.' Getting straight to it, I thought. 'I know I don't really have any right to get involved at this stage with your swimming or academic life, but I can see this beautiful and talented girl seemingly letting things slip through her fingers due to issues that could be sorted.' I wondered what part of my life could be sorted and how exactly they were going to sort it: would they get on the blocks and dive into the water with me? Kicking their legs out strong behind me like I used to? 'Look,' I started, 'I'm really sorry for how this is going to sound but I would like you to take it in objectively; it's not personal. I'm sick of talking about how I feel, and most of all I'm sick of feeling the way I do.' I looked at him across the table of the low-lit restaurant. The days were getting shorter, and my patience was fading just like the receding light. – 'The reason I want to speak to you about it now is that if you come down on the 19th, I don't want to hassle you all day about it then.' I watched his calloused hands move on the table as he spoke. 'I want our time together to be fun and we don't have to talk about stuff that could upset you – our time is precious enough as it is. You have been a major part of my life for so many years and although I know we are so different in many ways, I will always think of you as a daughter, and as a father I need to help you.' He looked at me earnestly. It was strange how they all wanted to force me back into the water; it seemed like everyone was in on it.

Behind me the waitress was lighting candles and setting them on a tray as she went and I had half turned around to watch her. The exposed beams and exposed brick made sound jump around the room strangely as a chair scraped back on the small mezzanine above us and echoed in the far corner. 'Can I ask, what is going on in your head at the moment? I can only go on what your mum tells me, but I want to know from you,' he interrupted my inspection. – 'I know and understand that you are offering help,' I looked down and picked my thumb as I said it, 'but I don't want to talk about it any more than I did in the first place.' I let my eyes come up to meet his; I could see he was getting frustrated. – 'You have a natural talent for swimming and academia and up until now you seem to have been able to do both to a very high standard, but do you feel you can still do both? If not, which of them is going to lose? I know your academic work is most important to you, but you have an Olympic Games with your name on it – it will come and then it'll be gone, finished,' he said. I said nothing in response, determined not to be moved by these hollow pleas. 'Please let's chat about these things. It is very important that your years of determination, focus and sacrifice are not belittled by some of the things that have happened, that in a few years may look like drops in the ocean.' He was really pleading now, pleading with me to tell him something, or rather, as I secretly believed, no one wanted me to say anything; they just wanted me to go back and swim and pretend that I'd never confessed I didn't want to anymore. If he knew, if he could feel only a small percentage of the humiliation I had endured over the years, I questioned whether or not he would still be asking this of me, or if in fact this was just what people said when they didn't understand at all, but they thought they had to say something.

'I don't feel . . .' I had to stop straight away to clear my throat, because feelings hadn't passed my lips much lately. 'I don't feel that it's anyone's place to tell me that I am letting something slip through my fingers. What I do in terms of swimming and academia is my choice alone. I am well aware of the sacrifices I've made, and also how this decision I might make will shape my future,' I exhaled deeply as I finished. It was exhausting shaping the words, connecting them to my thoughts and then trying to make them make sense when I said them out loud.

'But I don't want you to lose what you have worked so hard to get,' he said. I could feel all the brittle tendons in my body, all screaming at once: is this what I worked so hard to get? 'I think you really need to ask yourself some hard questions—' I was barely listening anymore. '—and clear the fog.' My life, in that moment, really felt like it had only ever been people telling me what to do. 'Imagine 2012 and you are sitting at home, watching the Olympics, instead of being there; would you be really happy that you had let the chance to finish your dream slip? It may not be your only dream, but if it is still a dream, you have the capability to realise it. If you still want it and want it badly, you can be an Olympian. Can you imagine what that will do for you in your life?' This time it was my chair scraping back, and it took us both a while to realise because the sound reverberated on the other side of the room before it came back to the floor beneath me. I could imagine exactly what that would do for me in my life. 'I have made my decision,' I said, my jaw burning. 'It is for no one else to tell me what I have to do.' I didn't know if I believed myself as I said it. I went on, 'Hard work is never wasted. I didn't swim my whole life just to make the Olympics. Swimming has never just been about the outcome.'

On the slow walk home through the new city I didn't know I got out my phone to send him a message. 'I'm sorry' was all I could manage. It was almost September and summer felt far behind. Once more, I was alone, in a new place, at a new school and a new swimming club. On the walk I passed a chapel on a long road that ended in a war memorial. The organ sounded through the walls and the bricks sang. I remembered Dan singing 'Jerusalem' in the inter-house music competition back in Plymouth with a single spotlight illuminating his promise and his perfect nose casting a shadow across the side of his face that might betray him. His voice had filled the assembly hall, deep and cracking as the melody swelled. Like the marble pool in Rome, his beauty in that moment haunted me still; pure and perfect, we were so untouchable then. These memories haunted my dreams too; in them we were chased by a pack of wolves that became naked people; they turned like a herd of horses – chest and body before head – and, unthinking, they galloped after us, and when they realised there was nothing more to see they turned back. Dan was in prison now. He had gone back up north when he'd left school and swimming hadn't been enough to carry him away from the life that had always been waiting for him at the end of that song. There aren't many people who can achieve their dreams, Paul had said in the restaurant. 'Is the Olympics still your dream?' he'd asked. I didn't know. Was the Olympics ever our dream, or was it just a dream we were told we had, like memories from a childhood created from stories about places you'd never been but wished you'd visited?

Almost a month later, after I'd come back from another late training session, I left a message for Paul: 'Just trying to call you but I realised I don't have your home phone number and it's the wrong time of night to try and get you on your mobile . . . I'll try again tomorrow if that's okay. Things have been a bit messy lately and everything's been up and down, I'm drained and completely exhausted after this week but my mock exams start on the 11th so I'm trying to get myself sorted.' I wondered if this was too long a message to leave. 'It's really hard to explain everything without talking to you face-to-face, so I won't try to. I would love to see you – revision isn't going fantastically, but I do have a lot of time at the moment anyway, so please, please let me know and I will see what we can sort out, even if it's only a day. Maybe you could call me tomorrow. It would be great to have a chat as I feel I haven't spoken to you for ages. Missing you so much, lots of love.' I pulled the phone down to my chest when I finished and held my feelings there. That night, in warm-up, I'd cried into my goggles like I used to do when I was young. The mirrored film protected my tears from everyone else and I let the sorrow fall and collect in salty pools in the small caps over my eyes. Unlike when I was young, I didn't finish the session feeling any differently. Who was I? A girl who didn't know what she was or who she wanted to be. My bitterness at this cliché prevented the catharsis of my body in the water or the relief of the tears from my ducts. The next morning, training came, and I got up and got my bag and waited near the corner shop in the dark to be picked up by another swimmer's parents and driven to the pool on the other side of the city. Before school, I had a voicemail message on my phone: 'You must be in turmoil at the moment.' It was Paul. 'Your mum has spoken to me about how seriously you're talking about this and there must be loads of things going on in your head. I hear you may really be giving up swimming? This must be a very difficult subject to talk about as it's you who is at the centre of it all. It's difficult to step outside the box and see the situation, especially if you are in the middle of it all, but everyone around you wants you to be happy in your life and everyone wants you to achieve your goals. Honest, it's not for them, it is for you.' His voice was gruff, short and hard like his filed-down teeth, and I wanted to cry again.

Everywhere I went I saw the edge of the world. And I felt it when I closed my eyes. Nothing was real except for my loneliness. If I fell over the edge, maybe someone would notice, and they'd come and get me and take me somewhere nice, with soft clothes and low lighting and food that I didn't have to have a relationship to. I was sitting at the dining-room table watching the toaster when Mum came in and asked me if I really needed to have another piece of toast. 'I have an eating disorder,' I said almost automatically. 'I don't know why you think you can say things like that to me.' I think she knew I was throwing up, but I didn't know that she was so ill-equipped to deal with it. Everything I did was exhaustingly calculated, because for the first time in as long as I could remember I was deciding to do it myself. Being instructed to swim so hard I threw up had been so customary that deciding to stick my fingers down my own throat to the same outcome didn't seem strange at all. What was strange, however, was the fact that I had to make the decision myself; it made it feel fake. Anything I could control seemed so flimsy and inconsequential after having had so little ceded to me for so long. Nothing I could do to myself could compare to what other people had made me do, and what I'd done because I'd thought they wanted me to. Mum left the kitchen, and later that afternoon I heard her talking on the phone in the room at the top of the house. 'I don't know if it was that episode with that prick Roan or if she's just burnt-out,' I heard her say sharply. 'No, no,' she interrupted the voice on the other side of the phone, 'I know, but if it's not that serious, she needs to get some focus back and try to look ahead a couple of years.' Then I could tell she was listening intently. 'Exactly, imagine where she could be . . .' The conversation trailed off as I heard her walk to the other side of the room and the thick pile carpet insulated her urgent tone. A lot of people were talking about me; it could have been any number of conspirators talking into that phone with my mother. Everyone seemed to be done listening and they wanted me to 'stop it'. I'd been back in the pool for almost two months now, and some part of me was hoping I'd snap out of it as well. I wondered if I might be used up. Maybe seventeen long years submerged in deep water was all I had in me and I was all dried-up, like a man-made well whose pump had broken and there wasn't any more water to tap beneath me anyway. Every day I took these thoughts with me and went to training.

'What is causing you trouble with your swimming?' It was the headmistress at my new school. We were sitting across from each other in her underwhelming office in the main L-shaped block of the new school building. Through the large window behind her there was a green courtyard with large limestone flags marking a path towards a giant silver sunflower – a sculpture and also a water feature. I watched the trickle of the clear liquid that fell slowly under no pressure down the sunflower's stem, so slowly it looked almost viscous, like vodka. 'It's not a problem if you're burnt-out, you know,' she paused for effect. 'If you are, then you are still you, and we all believe in you and what you're capable of inside and outside the pool; but whatever your decision, you need to be clear.' – 'Thank you, Miss,' I said robotically. – 'If you have serious problems and don't want to talk about them at home or with your coach, well, I hope you can talk to me,' she probed further.

What did they all think I was going to say? That I had reached a natural plateau, and I wasn't sure I could go beyond it? Or that all the change in my life over the last couple of years have left me empty, depleted and that performing is about confidence and mine was in pieces? I looked to the left beyond her to where the water was collecting at the sunflower's metal roots, which had been fashioned like a stand and were holding it upright. I didn't want to do it anymore. I laughed as I thought about saying it out loud. I imagined how Roan would have laughed in my face, with a nasty snarl in his top lip. I could have pleaded, but I had too much pride for that. I'd cried instead to my mum, to my old coach in London, to my godparents, to Julia. I would even cry now, in this office, if I thought that would work. I wasn't a child who didn't want to play the clarinet anymore, I was an athlete: an object, a hero story, and people had spent too much to let me go without a fight.

XXIV

I had never been skiing before and I didn't want anyone to know that. There were still so many things I had never done, a fact I had become acutely aware of after the way my world had opened up over the past year. As part of an effort to keep everyone training right up until Christmas, Julia had decided a training camp was in order: we were going for a week to a small resort in Austria. We would ski in the day and swim at a local pool in the town each morning and evening. Julia believed in life, and she believed in risk and living while swimming, especially at this level. She was realistic about where we were: not in Plymouth anymore. This swimming club was never going to take me to the Olympics, and my going on this training camp was an acceptance of that fact. The threat and fear of injury was so constant that we weren't allowed to run, or even walk around that much during the run-up to big competitions; no playing pick-up football, or a little tennis on holiday in case you landed wrong and sprained an ankle or pulled the delicate tendons across the top of your foot. If I went skiing, I could break my leg, so, yes, this really was the end.

Up on the slopes on the first day, I avoided ski school by saying I'd skied before. The altitude formed a mist that dropped the visibility down so low my stomach dropped with it as we travelled up over the mountain. I didn't know the cold would drain my phone battery straight away, or how to hold my sticks on the lift. At the top, I hoped there was another way down, but there wasn't. Everything around us was white. When I was younger, on our long veranda in Nairobi, I used to rollerblade up and down its length with my dark blue swimming costume on. Now, I thought about the angle of my old rollerblades gripping down the steepness of the red run. I closed my eyes to make myself start and went down straight, so fast I thought I would never stop. My conscious brain had no idea how to move either. Somehow, my body pushed my skis together at the bottom, and I came to an abrupt standstill without falling, which had seemed completely impossible. We trained and our bodies hurt, mainly from the time on the mountain, then we slept hard and did it again.

I was certain there was another misstep around the corner. I walked gingerly through my days but threw myself down the slopes as if the world were ending. On the day that I was due to find out my exam results I checked Facebook to see if anyone else I had met at my Oxford interview had any good news to share. There was only one place for my subject at the college I had applied to, so if there was good news for someone else that meant bad news for me. The hotel rooms of the chalet were dark. Fake panelled walls lacquered thick with molasses-coloured varnish and dark blue rugs with matching blinds, dark like the future I could no longer see.

'I don't think I got in,' I said as soon as I picked up the phone. 'Why do you say that?' It was my mum, and I couldn't work out from her voice if she was trying to protect me by not yet confirming, or if she knew something else. 'One of the girls I was there with, you know, that one whose brother went there, she said it was easy when she came out of the final interview before me, and she messaged me, but I haven't read it.' 'I have the envelope,' Mum replied. 'It's quite thick.' I was silent while I considered that if all my self-worth had once been bound up in the pool, then it had to go somewhere else in order for me to carry on affirming my reality, and I needed this to catch me. 'Do you want me to wait until you get—' 'Open it,' I interrupted. – 'Are you sure? Because I know this is going to be hard if it's not . . .' Her words trailed off, and I knew it was because she didn't want to say it out loud: *if I didn't get in.* Other people wanted this, they had thought about it and decided it was for them, and I knew they were hungry and well trained and they hadn't missed half of their GCSE year or got a B in Maths or been told they were failing school when they got back from the Commonwealth Games with a look that said, 'I don't know why you're doing this to yourself.' I knew how badly others wanted it, but I needed it. 'We are pleased to inform you . . .' my mum started to read. I looked at the dark blue wallpaper, peeling at the corner against the stained skirting board. Relief is the absence of fear, I understood then, not the addition of anything good.

Someone took a picture at the beginning of the night. I was wearing dark lipstick and lots of eyeliner, with flushed cheeks from alcohol, snow and excitement. My knitted bright red headband concealed unkempt edges and extensions gave me a messy ponytail. I looked seventeen – I finally looked my age in a way I never had done before, because I was doing exactly what everyone else my age was doing. At the back of the bar people were smoking. One of the ski instructors from earlier in the week offered me a lighter and I almost set my hair on fire; the synthetic strands burned like plastic Tupperware. I didn't react because it wasn't real, but he didn't know that and looked at me strangely for the rest of the evening. I wanted to recover my whole youth: to drink underage and inconvenience people, to take a lighter from a stranger even though I didn't know how to smoke, and to get carried home because I couldn't stand up by myself. That night I drank to fill the space where fear had been, and I could feel an emptiness bubbling up inside me. The next morning, before we were allowed to go up the slopes again, I had swimming training at the small five-lane pool a mile walk from our chalet. I struggled through the session hungover; swimming was no longer compatible with the way I was treating my body or what I thought my future looked like. Without those clearly defined parameters, everything in my life slowed down; my relationship with time changed and I learned boredom for the first time, a feeling I'd never really known. And I liked it – but mostly I felt empty, and when I got back home to Oxford, I began to understand that there were so many hours in a day to feel nothing.

To mark the end, I took my fake ID to a tattoo parlour on Queen Street. I was twisted over as he finished the date, my left hip stacked on top of my right, propped up and leaning my head on my right hand. '22/12/11', the words it followed meandered around my hip bone in two lines and came to a halt before the top of my pelvis. My skin burned, and I told myself it didn't hurt because I was preparing to tell other people that it hadn't. I turned the words over in my head. The soft hum of the electric needle ceased, and tiny pinhead beads of blood were left on its metallic surface which I saw in the reflection of the window, as well as the words etched into my body back to front. As I was getting dressed, I turned to the man who was now cleaning off the tattoo gun. 'If I lose weight, will it affect the way it looks?' I asked self-consciously. He grunted in assent. I still felt unattached to my body. Outside, the cold could be seen condensing on the windows of the double-deckers, as the passengers' warm breath mingled with the almost freezing air. Beyond the bus stop, cobbles differentiated the college's entrance from the pavement, the flow of traffic moved the working people towards the end of town and further outside the ring road. This distinction between pavement and original cobbles seemed enough to encapsulate the whole of the city. This is not your path anymore, it said: this is a private place, it's not for you and it never will be.

In some ways the college looked like the grey Tudor castle of the original school building in Plymouth, but my eyes were now trained to know better. The heavy wooden doors, large enough for a two-horse carriage, were surrounded by patchwork stone and charming crags whose greying colour would be sand-blasted down to reveal the golden hue of their original splendour, which I had seen glowing in the late summer evenings earlier that year. I wondered if one day it would all be gone, sand-blasted away, and the whole city would look like Rome – craters of relics of an ancient elitism that in pursuit of perfection slowly eroded its own form. But because those heavy wooden doors, all of them, were always so firmly closed – there was no fragility in them – and even though the city was made up of these monuments, they had no real interaction, as buildings, with this place at all.

The next Tuesday, I told my mum I wasn't going back to training for the last time; I'd been trying to quit for over a year. The torture of trudging to the pool for those last couple of months in Oxford was worse than anything I'd forced myself to do before. Some days I turned up at morning training drunk. I'd crept out the night before, out of my skylight window that opened onto the street from my lower ground-floor room and out with new friends who had no idea what I did in the pool because I didn't want that to be my identity anymore. Julia could see that I was done, and I guess she'd been able to for a long time, because we both knew what we'd lived through at Plymouth. She was the only one who really let me go with dignity. She knew what Roan was like, how it felt as if he'd got inside my mind and put his big hand around my brain and squeezed and squeezed and squeezed until the cord that connected it to my spine and ran down to my pelvis and connected my legs to my hips had given way and snapped. There was no more strong breaststroke kick, there was no more strong anything. There was just me, and I wanted to get out of the pool. I wanted to get out all the time, I wanted to get out and I never wanted to get back in again. That I had put one foot in front of the other since the Europeans still felt like a miracle to me, but I had been a zombie for much of the last year and a half, throwing up in private, shoulders hunched in public, trying as much as possible to get out of training. One day back in London, I'd turned up to the morning session and instead of going out onto poolside, even though my coach had already seen me walk in, I went into one of the changing-room stands and locked the door and lay on the cold, tiled floor for two hours, until dawn broke and it was 7.30 a.m., and then I went to school. I was so done I needed a new word for it: when I tried to say it out loud it didn't even feel like I was speaking English. Or maybe I hadn't said it out loud, maybe I hadn't even said it to myself? But I had; I'd said it to myself a thousand times and to everyone else at least a hundred of those. I had to fight my way out of the pool like I'd fought my way in. Scared and shaking, with my mother's hands holding the rubber ring around my waist and the blow-up armbands tight around my soon-to-be-biceps, not yet ribbed with strong muscles. She'd held me then, when the water hadn't felt like home. The water wasn't home anymore, but I knew I had to get out by myself.

Grief came like paralysis. For the three days that followed, I was silent and watchful. And every day I saw the exact moment the streetlamps came on in the evening and watched them go off again at dawn. What did people do with all this time? It hit me immediately, as overnight my days had doubled in length: the half-hour to the pool, two and a half on poolside, land warm-up then swim, get changed, then the half-hour back. My days had six more hours to them. I wondered how it could ever be possible to not do your homework. I was listless and mourning. Not chronologically, in stages, but all at once: denial, depression, anger, bargaining, more anger, rage. In order to walk away from my sport, I had told myself that it wasn't worth it, that to stand on that podium or even swim another length I would have to pay too high a price. I wanted to choose for myself the life that I would live – the life I could live – but I wasn't ready for that choice to set off an explosion and the shrapnel tore straight through me, tearing through the hours, blasting them apart and away from one another until time moved so slowly, I could hear myself blink. Nothing felt autonomous. Every breath was like having my mouth open underwater, and I was screaming silently. The shrapnel also tore a hole in my head; where joy and lightness and adrenaline had cohabited, now there was nothing. I thought about how much I had hated training at the end, and how this was so much worse than that. Then, I waited for the hours to get shorter. They didn't. But slowly I became more able to tolerate them. As the year ended, so did my swimming career, and still the strangest thing of all was that this was not the end of my life.

*

Each day I chose a different road to cut through and across the two main arteries that led away from town to get towards the river and my school. The January days were cold and every place I went was cold too. With the fingers of my right hand balanced lightly on the join at the middle of the handlebars, I cycled slowly and upright. There were no leaves and no light on the road. There was no light anywhere. Suddenly, a car reversed out of a driveway right in front of me at speed, without looking. My left hand was immediately on my brake, my right hand straight out in front of me as the back wheel of my bike lifted off the surface of the road and started to travel in an arc towards me. The car braked hard as my front wheel stopped just short of its undercarriage and my hand hit the red paint-work between its windows. I stopped too, unscathed. I loved being alive. I always had: it's why I've always been so scared, full of fear and ready to fight. I realised then that this fear would take me everywhere – anywhere I wanted to go, because there is no will without fear, no will to reach beyond the limit to a place that other people didn't believe existed. Fear took me towards it always, and I was travelling forward still. And I would keep going.

At the end of the road, I looked left and right. Beyond the traffic lights was the turning that would have taken me on to the pool and the training session that would already be long over that morning I pushed forward instead and cycled straight across, and as I reached the other side, I thought about everything I had given to that part of my life, and also what it had taken from me. It was still hard to breathe. Through all those years in the water, I'd lost my innocence about people and their promises of safety, and I'd lost my innocence about the colour of my skin. I'd left it all at the bottom of a swimming pool. But I had also been the best: for a short moment, I knew what it felt like to be able to do something better than anyone else, and I would do it all again just to feel that. As the bitterness swelled, I breathed in the morning and the memory of the perfect race. I took my hands off the handlebars and remembered how lucky I was to have flown so close to the sun and let my brown skin bask in its rays, and as the low light of sunrise crested the bare trees, I felt it all subside.

Epilogue

Through the early months that summer of 2012, the second thought I had most days was of my results. What it would feel like if I got my grades and got into Oxford, and the horror of what I would do if I didn't. After my final exam, I got a job at a café and my shifts there punctuated the weeks, offering respite from the endless hours of my new days; no longer filled with training, they refused to pass me by. One morning, I woke up thinking of a long essay question at the end of my second politics paper. It was just before 6 a.m., which meant I'd had just less than two hours of sleep. A durable insomnia promised to meet my anxious mind every night and last night had been no exception. At 3 a.m. the frustration would start to wash away. The loneliness of those early-morning hours was the only time anything seemed to make sense, when my reality mirrored my internal world; that I was completely alone, there was no one to turn to, no one there and no one coming. Everyone slept through my pain, oblivious to the city that was slowly falling down inside me as my identity crumbled and fell away, no longer *the swimmer*, and every night at 4 a.m., my stinging eyes and the absolute silence told me that my pain was real and that for now, without the relief of sleep, there was no way out.

In a small pile next to a full-length French antique mirror was a pair of gym shorts, a white racer-back sports bra and a pair of bright blue Brooks trainers. I pulled running socks from the top draw of the dresser at the end of my bed and got changed in the semi-darkness of my lower-ground-floor bedroom. Soft, diffuse light and fading birdsong mingled outside and I took the stairs three at a time, lunging to stretch out my hip flexors as I walked up towards the landing. Our small kitchen faced the smaller back garden looking onto the river. I hated this house: slightly plastic, uninspiring and full of disappointment. I took a large glass bottle from the fridge, meant for the table at dinner. It was filled with cold water, and I drank it all in one go. As I refilled it, I washed my face over the kitchen sink then replaced the bottle. Taking another, I repeated the process. This was one of the healthier compulsions I'd developed, but I still knew that some days I was probably dangerously close to drowning myself.

Out on the quiet street I rotated my ankles anticlockwise, pushing my toes into the pavement for purchase and twisting my tendons to warm them up. The few people I saw watched me as I ran past; I was barely clothed and despite it being summer it was too cold to be wearing so little, but when they looked, I ran faster, arms pumping, face soft but serious, self-conscious, stride wide and toes light on the tarmac. I ran on the road into town, down the main high street, round the Radcliffe Camera and back again. As the morning lightened the roads got busier, and the more people there were around, the faster I ran. I sprinted the last 200 metres, all the way to our door, and looked down at my watch: five kilometres, eighteen minutes, lungs burning and the faint memory of unimaginable pain, no relief. No matter how fast I ran, or how much impressed acknowledgement my spectators provided, the high was always subtle, the euphoria fleeting.

Pride is a hugely defining part of any winning athlete. When you've won so much, it's hard to lose: it's physically painful; your psyche can't handle it. Some people want to be carried out, to swim until they can't anymore, their broken body ushering in the end. I needed to walk out, I had to. Staying until I couldn't win anymore had felt like a death sentence – but my current purgatory, as it turned out, was worse. My life had become a constant inner monologue. I couldn't stop the thoughts, and all the feelings I'd drowned out for years and years, all the things I'd emptied from my head again and again. All the fear from my childhood, all the uncertainty, it came back all at once. It was too much to contain, and there wasn't enough serotonin in the world to keep me from sinking. The fear, as it turned out, was about being ordinary. 'What if we are all the same?' I asked myself. How could this pain be meaningful if I could have lived without it and ended up exactly where I was now? This is the kind of fatalism you think will never leave. It does, but not before you've spent months questioning. I was snarling at the bars of the cage of my plain life as I disappeared into a sea of unextraordinary people, wondering why I had spent so much time training and learning to be otherwise. Success is just a set of ingredients. It's easy to believe that you've been gifted them, but you haven't. They aren't yours.

Maybe you're lucky and you start off with one or two, but the rest are just a material result of the choice to remove all friction from your life. You don't have sleepovers or get drunk in the park in your early teens, no house parties or stealing your parents' alcohol; concentrating in biology class is also low priority, doing your homework even lower – all these frictions will stop you from achieving greatness. That is the only way. And then, even after you've removed all of these obstacles from your path, your conscious mind still stands in your way. A thousand sacrifices might never be enough if you can't win the inner game too, can't quiet your thoughts enough to let your body take control.

When I got back from my run, I wrapped my hair in a purple and dark blue cotton headscarf to stop the post-run sweat seeping from my hairline to my brows and sat on my bedroom floor for an hour with my eyelids lightly closed, meditating. This couldn't be it: I had to believe that I could control it; if I ran more, ate less, focused harder, I wouldn't feel like this forever. And if this was it, I wasn't going down without a fight. I had no words for how I was feeling, even though my head was full of the ugliest thoughts I'd ever had, but they had no shape, no vowels or consonants, no grammar to make intelligible the sadness I carried around in my chest, my stomach, my head. My strong legs transported this despair through my now empty days; it was like carrying an 80-kilogram barbell everywhere I went. Together with this weight I was also finally learning the lesson of adulthood: no one was coming to make it better. It's like getting too old to hold onto the trolley your parent is pushing at the supermarket and being too self-conscious to put your hand on your younger sibling's pushchair as you walk alongside. Your hand on this object tethers you to a soothing comfort that allays your fears; you're physically connected to the somebody who will protect you from bad things happening, and even when they're not there, you still believe it. Some days I ran, some days I binged, most days I threw up. 'Why can't you help me?' I thought as I made myself sick in the toilet before I went to work. I suppose I was talking to my mother. I wanted her to make it better, but without realising I had long ago taken my hand away, or my swimming had taken me away from the comfort of her. Object permeance. We learn to trust that the things we can't see are still there; but sometimes they aren't anymore.

At 5 p.m. I walked the five minutes home from the café with my apron over my shoulder, my hands smelling of coffee and my breath of cigarettes. I had taken to smoking Superking Benson & Hedges in my breaks at work and sometimes late at night when my parents had gone to bed. Never socially, always alone. I didn't know why; it was something different and something intense, it kept me full. I liked the headrush and the solitude, the meditativeness of the moment, the smell of smoke and the self-possessing drama of it all. After I got through the door I immediately wanted to run again. I was sure I'd breached my daily calorie threshold. I didn't have a problem with food, I promised myself this obsessively, I wasn't trying to disappear; I was just trying to train myself out of wanting to eat the 5,000 calories a day I'd consumed almost every day for the past six years. I was terrified of putting on weight. I told myself this was also legitimate; yes, I had an eating disorder, but it was rooted in hard science: 5,000 calories in, two measly 5-kilometre runs at less than 500 calories each, so that's 2,000 calories burned from being alive, 1,000 from running like a maniac, which still, if I allowed my appetite to run unchecked, left 2,000 extra calories consumed and unaccounted for each day. Even if I ran every day, which I didn't, that was 14,000 extra calories a week. I'd worked out that if I let myself, I was going to steadily put on a stone each month. I was starving.

In the shower I could hear my mother calling me for dinner. I had timed it perfectly. I put my head under the running water to drown out her voice, tipping my chin down towards my collarbones and letting the water run down from behind my ears as I watched it travel in rivers over my nipples and collect at the top of the still-defined V-shape of muscles that framed my pelvis before disappearing between my legs. I padded my damp feet down two flights of carpeted stairs, closed the door behind me and dropped my towel in front of the mirror in my room. I tensed my arms by my sides and watched my lats rise in manly diamonds around my neck. The definition of my abs was almost completely gone, and I sucked in my ribs and arched my back to bring a faint line down the middle of my stomach; not great, I thought. Turning to my side, I ran my hand down from the small of my back to the softest part of the very top of the back of my leg, where it met my bum. I tensed and released and did it again; my bum was falling, definitely. I pulled at the beginnings of mottled cellulite. Even though the sound had been coming through the open window for a while, I was doing my best to dissociate from the mounting reality of this moment: I was sitting in my bedroom and on the TV upstairs all the competitors for the final of the 100-metre breaststroke had just been announced. Somewhere beyond Hackney, in a brand-new pool I'd never seen, my event was about to be swum at the Olympic Games. 'Are you going to come upstairs?' My mother's voice penetrated my dissociative state. She was trying to be there for me. I pretended not to hear her again. But after the cheering I could hear the unmistakable sound of the beginning of a race, silence, then the second whistle, also unmistakable. The buzzer, the splash.

65.47 seconds. I held my breath for all of them. In just over a minute their race was over, and in the split second before it ended, despite not watching, I understood exactly what was going to happen. There had been a girl, younger than me, that I had trained with in Plymouth for a month over the summer before I left, and she was going to out-touch the American for Olympic gold. And all I could think about was how insignificant that period of my life was, how quickly it had changed since I had quit, but that this was nothing compared to how quickly hers would. Olympic champion, it's forever. I didn't know what forever meant anymore. 'I can't believe it,' I could hear my mother saying; my stepdad asked her something, but she didn't answer. I put my headphones on and replayed a crooning folksy ballad over and over again. My door handle

turned, and I quickly turned off the lights. 'Are you okay?' she
paused, and then, 'I can smell smoke', my mother said, but
she stayed at the top of the stairs. She meant: are *you* okay?
My pain was also hers, as it always had been. 'It's incense,' I
replied, my heart racing as she closed the door and I put out
the cigarette. 'I'm going to sleep,' I shouted up after her. Twenty
minutes later when the TV was finally turned off, I turned my
lights back on and lay on my back on the carpet. My parents
were moving around above me, each of them identifiable,
distinguished by things only I could hear. My mother's silver
bangles touched lightly when she took the first step upstairs.
They created the softest of chimes, like Italian church bells
stuffed into a sleeping bag. Next, as always, my stepdad went
to get them some water. He held the two glasses together
between the thumb and forefinger of his left hand and used
his right to reach for the banister. The glasses chimed as well.
The second bell toll, but this time a single note higher. He
followed my mother upstairs, and I was alone in the bottom
of the house.

The strange window-like door that opened onto a small
ladder that ran up to street level was still slightly ajar. I thought
about listening to that same song again for the twentieth time
that day, crouching in the lightwell and smoking another cigarette. Instead, I reached for a book I'd been re-reading obsessively
since I'd been given it by one of my parents' friends to prepare
for my Oxford interviews at the end of last year. 'In the end,
we are self-perceiving, self-inventing, locked-in mirages that are
little miracles of self-reference.' 'I am a strange loop,' I whispered

to myself in the silence. My Black genes held within themselves a thousand little copies, concertinaed like coastlines, renewing and repeating, but always the same. My thoughts like caves within caves within caves. I am a strange loop. Maybe one day I will meet myself again at the very beginning, and instead of this watery world taking me in its jaws, I will, instead, swallow myself whole.

Acknowledgements

With huge thanks to my informal proposal editors, Rita and Francesca, as well as my very real editor Helena, all at Canongate, and also my indescribably incredible agent, Victoria: you have all made this real for me. Thanks again to Rita and also Aiden – I wrote much of this book in your apartment; thank you for listening to me and laughing with me, I am indebted to your generosity. Thanks to Mica, for telling me to write this in the first place and Finn, for making sure I actually did. Frank, thank you for holding my words through this. Thank you, Seren and Anthony, for being with me in the pool then and in my life now; thank you for telling me the truth and helping me to hold onto it. My family, you've suffered with and for me. I am with you always. My father, I wish I knew you enough to miss you like a daughter. I miss you like I miss my ancestors; your pride guides me everywhere. And, Mumma, you've kept my soul safe all these years and you will forever, thank you for loving me so fiercely.

This book is for all of you as much as it is for me.

And to all the Black and brown bodies in the water, this is also for you, and I love you all.